The Wooden Spoon
Book
of Old Family Recipes

The Wooden Spoon Book
of Old Family Recipes

from The Wooden Spoon Kitchen

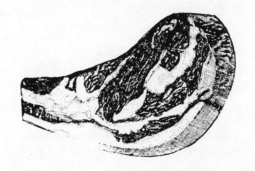

Marilyn M. Moore

THE ATLANTIC MONTHLY PRESS

NEW YORK

Published simultaneously in Canada
Printed in the United States of America

FIRST PAPERBACK EDITION

The previous edition of this book was catalogued by the Library of Congress as follows:

Moore, Marilyn M.
Meat and potatoes and other comfort foods from the wooden spoon kitchen /Marilyn M. Moore. — 1st ed.
Includes bibliographical references and index.
1. Cookery (Meat)   2. Cookery (potatoes)   I. Title.
TX749.M573   1995   641.5—dc20   95-992

0-87113-694-5

Design by Laura Hammond Hough

The Atlantic Monthly Press
841 Broadway
New York, NY 10003

10 9 8 7 6 5 4 3 2 1

For my favorite meat and potatoes cooks:
DIANE, JEANETTE, AND SELMA

Acknowledgments

Heartfelt thanks to:

Ilse Fliesser and Jessie Boyd for sharing recipes with me.

Mardee Haidin Regan for her shared editing expertise.

The Pork Information Bureau and the National Pork Producers Council for information on trichinosis.

The National Livestock and Meat Board for information on cuts of meat.

Contents

Desserts 165

Introduction

I was winding up work on a project when Anton Mueller of Atlantic Monthly Press called to ask if I might consider doing a meat and potatoes cookbook. What timing! I asked a few questions to define what he was thinking and discovered that he basically wanted me to write a book about what I enjoy cooking and how I do it, so that you, the reader, can follow suit.

The outline I devised for my own purposes was for a book I could have written without leaving my computer keyboard. I didn't do that, of course, because it's in the execution of a recipe that you remember the insights that must be passed on. A recipe that is a listing of ingredients with sparse methods is fine for the accomplished chef but not sufficient for an everyday home cook. So, there was the usual process of writing, testing, correcting, testing again, and so on, until I felt that someone else could follow the directions and come up with approximate results.

Although the recipes list exact measurements, this is not the way the experienced usually cook. Measuring in the palm of one's hand is more likely than measuring with a spoon. Let me encourage you to do the same, altering my work as you see fit. As you gain confidence in the kitchen you will learn to trust your own instincts for how much of an herb or spice to use on any given day.

I have always said that I didn't want to write a low-fat cookbook, but, without realizing it, I have gradually limited the fats I use. You can't make an honest french-fried potato without using fat, but there are many places where fats can be cut. I have noticed that some of my recipes turn out to be lower in fat than many I find in "diet" books. Others (like the french fry) are not. This mirrors the dichotomy of my daily kitchen. I suggest that rather than obsessing about diets and fats all of the time, you simply eat a little less than your capacity. Soon after a meal you may find that you are completely satisfied.

On the subject of fats: I use both butter (supposed to be bad for you) and olive oil (said to be good for you) because of their superior flavor. When I want an oil with little flavor, I use extra-light olive oil (no less fat, but milder taste). The oils I fry with are canola oil and corn oil. I sauté with olive oil or butter or a combination of the two. None of us can live without fats altogether, and a small amount in the diet can contribute to good health. The important thing to remember is that if you don't go overboard on fats, you can enjoy those french fries now and then.

Most of these recipes are tried and true standbys. You won't find daring new combinations of ingredients (that probably shouldn't be linked together in the first place). You will find directions to make a good home-cooked meal for your friends and family—what Anton calls "comfort food."

Some of my recipes use shortcuts. I don't mean that I cook with a can opener tied to my apron, but I will use a processed product if I like the results it produces. Everyone is busy these days, and it is unrealistic to expect cooks to make everything from scratch. A word of caution: Some of the recipes have "simple" included in the title. This does not mean the dish can be done in 10 minutes or less, but that the methods have been simplified over what standard recipes would specify.

As I worked on my outline, I kept thinking of recipes that had to be included, and how long it had been since I had made open-faced hamburgers, roasted a chicken, or fixed pot roast. It seems I had gotten into a rut with my cooking, as I imagine many of you have. Thank you, Anton, for getting me out of my rut. The book has been fun, and if you, dear reader, are in a rut with your cooking, perhaps thumbing through it will help you climb out of yours.

Meats on the Hoof

When a family member asks, "What's for dinner?" don't be fooled into thinking they want to know all about your salads, vegetables, breads, or desserts. What they are really asking is, "What's the meat?" When they sit down at the table they may dig in to the side dishes planned to complement the choice of meat, but it's not what they want to hear about. Next time you're asked the question, answer with one of the mouthwatering favorites found in this chapter.

To impress, serve Standing Rib Roast with Yorkshire Pudding, Beef Bourguignonne, Roast Beef Tenderloin, Veal Scallopini, or Roast Rack of Lamb; for more relaxed dining, try Pan-Fried Steaks, Chinese Pepper Steak, London Broil, Simple Pot Roast with Gravy, Stuffed Pork Chops with Milk Gravy, or Oven-Barbecued Ribs with Homemade Barbecue Sauce; for easy family meals, make Sloppy Joes, Open-Faced Hamburgers, Fruited Beef Brisket, Braised Lamb Shanks, or Ham and Potato Pancakes.

Standing Rib Roast with Yorkshire Pudding

A standing rib roast is a treat usually reserved for special occasions. Why not go all the way and produce a Yorkshire pudding to go with it? Don't be intimidated by either the roast or the pudding. They're both reasonably easy to prepare.

There are always some diners who prefer their roast beef rare to medium-rare, and others who want it medium-well-done. Since the interior of the roast stays cool the longest, it is possible to produce slices that range from rare to almost well-done from the same piece of meat. The trick is to time the meat by inserting a meat thermometer in the thickest part of the center of the roast, away from any fat or bone. When that part registers rare, the roast is ready to come from the oven. Don't delay, as it will continue to cook while waiting to be carved.

The Yorkshire pudding should go into the oven soon after the roast comes out. By the time the roast is carved and all the plates are served, the pudding will be puffed and ready to make its glorious appearance.

SERVES 6 TO 8

STANDING RIB ROAST:
1 standing rib roast cut from the small end (4 to 4½ pounds)
salt and pepper

YORKSHIRE PUDDING:
1 cup bread flour
¾ teaspoon salt
1 cup milk
3 large eggs

1. Remove the roast from refrigeration 1 hour before roasting. Preheat the oven to 450°F.

2. Prepare the roast: Sprinkle salt and pepper on all sides of the roast; place, fat side up, in a shallow roasting pan, no rack is needed. Place in the oven and roast for 15 minutes.

3. Reduce the oven temperature to 350° and roast until a meat thermometer inserted in the center of the roast registers 140°, 45 to 60 minutes longer.

4. Transfer the roast to a platter and let rest for at least 15 minutes before carving. Reserve the drippings in the roasting pan. Increase the oven temperature to 400°.

5. Prepare the Yorkshire pudding: Spoon 3 tablespoons of the reserved drippings from the roasting pan into a 13×9-inch baking dish or pan. Place in the oven to preheat.

6. In a mixing bowl, whisk together the flour, salt, and milk until smooth. Add the eggs, 1 at a time, whisking well after each.

7. Remove the baking dish from the oven and swirl to coat the bottom with the melted fat. Pour the pudding batter into the pan and return to the oven. Bake for 20 minutes.

8. Reduce the oven heat to 350°, and bake until the pudding is puffed and browned, about 10 minutes longer.

Serving suggestion: Carve the roast into thin slices. Cut the pudding into squares. Defatted drippings from the roasting pan can be served in a small sauceboat on the side.

Roast Beef Tenderloin

A beef tenderloin is marvelous for entertaining. Put the meat in the oven when the guests arrive, and by the time they have enjoyed an appetizer and a welcoming glass of wine, the tenderloin is ready to serve.

SERVES 4 TO 6

1 beef tenderloin (2½ pounds)
salt and pepper
2 slices lean bacon

1. Let the meat stand at room temperature for 1 hour before cooking. Preheat the oven to 400°F.

2. Sprinkle the meat all over with salt and pepper. Lay the bacon slices over the roast. Place on a rack in a shallow roasting pan. Roast until a meat thermometer inserted in the center of the roast registers 130° for rare, 30 to 35 minutes. For medium-rare, roast to 145°, 40 to 45 minutes.

3. Let the roast stand for 10 minutes before slicing to serve.

Serving suggestion: Discard the bacon. Carve the meat into thin slices. Fan out 3 or 4 slices on each plate. Potatoes Anna is perfect with this dish.

Pan-Fried Steaks

The secret to pan-frying a steak that is tender, not tough, is to start with well-marbled meat, cook it quickly, and never, never let it stew in any liquid. Beware of "extra-lean" steaks in the meat case: Although they are sometimes hard to distinguish from beef that is more tender, they will not be labeled "choice."

I usually make this meal for only two. If you want to prepare it for four, you should plan to use a separate skillet for the additional steaks and prepare them all at the same time.

SERVES 2

1 tablespoon unsalted butter
2 rib-eye steaks, labeled "choice," cut about ¾ inch thick
    (12 ounces each)
salt and pepper
¼ cup dry red wine (optional)

1. Preheat the oven to 400°F.

2. Melt the butter in a large cast-iron or other ovenproof skillet over medium high to high heat (heating elements vary—you want to sear the steaks quickly without burning them). Sprinkle the steaks lightly on each side with salt and pepper; place in the skillet. Cook the steaks until browned on both sides, turning several times, 3 to 5 minutes (they will finish cooking in the oven).

3. Place the skillet in the oven to finish cooking to medium rare, 3 to 5 minutes. Cut into one of the steaks to test for doneness. Transfer the steaks to serving plates.

4. Pour the wine into the skillet. Cook on high, stirring often, until the liquid is reduced by about half, 2 to 3 minutes.

Serving suggestion: Pour the reduced wine over the steaks and serve immediately. Perfect with French-Fried Potatoes.

Chicken-Fried Steak with Cream Gravy

Properly fixed chicken-fried steak is a real taste treat. The meat has a mellow beef flavor shared by the creamy gravy.

SERVES 4

> *1½ pounds tenderized round steak*
> *salt and pepper*
> *½ cup all-purpose flour*
> *1 tablespoon extra-light olive oil*
> *2 tablespoons unsalted butter*
> *½ cup water*
> *½ cup light cream or half-and-half*

1. Cut the steak into 4 serving pieces. Trim away any fat from the edges. Working with 1 piece at a time, sprinkle salt and pepper and about 1 tablespoon flour over each side of the meat. Press the flour into the meat with your fingers, flattening the meat slightly.

2. Heat the oil and butter over medium-high heat in a skillet large enough to hold all of the meat at once. Add the meat and brown on both sides, turning once; remove the pieces as they are browned.

3. Pour off any remaining fat. Add the water to the skillet and stir to loosen any browned bits that stick to the pan. Return the steak to the liquid, reduce the heat, cover, and simmer until the steak is fork-tender, about 1 hour.

4. Remove the steak to a serving platter. Stir the cream into the gravy, taste and add salt and pepper if needed. Heat the gravy to just under boiling.

Serving suggestion: Spoon a little of the gravy over the meat and serve the remainder in a warmed sauceboat. Mom's Mashed Potatoes are essential with this dish.

Chinese Pepper Steak

I think Chinese Pepper Steak is more American than Chinese, but it makes great family fare.

SERVES 4

1 pound beef top round steak, cut 1 inch thick
2 tablespoons extra-light olive oil
1 medium onion, thinly sliced
1 garlic clove, minced or pressed
1 cup beef broth
¼ cup light soy sauce (be sure to use light soy sauce, or the dish will be too salty)
¼ teaspoon sugar
¼ teaspoon ground pepper
1 celery rib, sliced
1 large green bell pepper, cut into thin strips
1 can (14½ ounces) tomato wedges, drained
2 tablespoons cornstarch
¼ cup cold water

1. Slice the beef into strips, 2 to 3 inches long and ¼ inch wide. Heat 1 tablespoon of the oil in a skillet. Add the onion and garlic and cook over medium heat, stirring, until the onion is tender, 2 to 3 minutes. Remove to a side dish with a slotted spoon.

2. Add the remaining 1 tablespoon oil to the skillet. Add the beef in batches and sauté in the hot oil until browned on all sides, removing the pieces as they brown.

3. Add the broth, soy sauce, sugar, and ground pepper to the skillet; stir well. Return the beef, onion, and garlic to the skillet and reduce the heat. Cover and simmer for 20 minutes.

4. Add the celery, bell pepper, and tomatoes. Cover and cook until the celery and bell pepper are crisp-tender, about 5 minutes.

5. Dissolve the cornstarch in the cold water. Stir the mixture into the skillet, and cook, stirring constantly, until thickened, 1 to 2 minutes.

Serving suggestion: Spoon directly from the skillet. Good with Long-Grain or Brown Rice.

London Broil

London broil is flank steak that has been tenderized by crosscutting through some of the connective membranes that hold the meat together. If packages in the meat case are labeled "London Broil," then the butcher has already crosscut the meat. The steak should be grilled or broiled to no more than medium-rare to preserve that tenderness.

SERVES 4

1½ pounds London Broil or flank steak
1 tablespoon extra-virgin olive oil
1 tablespoon red wine vinegar
1 garlic clove, minced or pressed
salt and pepper

1. Preheat the broiler or get the grill ready to cook.

2. If you have purchased flank steak, cut a crisscross pattern on each side of the steak with a sharp knife. Mix together the oil, vinegar, and garlic; rub into the surface of the meat. Sprinkle both sides of the steak with salt and pepper.

3. Broil the steak 2 to 3 inches from the heat source, or grill over a hot fire until it is rare or medium rare, 5 to 7 minutes per side.

Serving suggestion: Slice the steak on the diagonal across the grain into ½-inch-thick slices. Perfect with Home-Fried Potatoes.

Swiss Steak

When you've had what passes for swiss steak at a charity function or two, it makes you hungry for the real thing. This should satisfy.

SERVES 4 TO 6

3 pounds heel of beef round, cut like a thick steak,
about 1½ inches thick
salt and pepper
½ cup all-purpose flour
2 tablespoons extra-virgin olive oil
2 onions, thinly sliced
1 can (28 ounces) tomatoes, with their juices

1. Preheat the oven to 325°F.

2. Cut the meat into serving pieces. Sprinkle the pieces with salt and pepper. Use the spiky side of a meat mallet★ to pound the flour into the pieces of meat.

3. In a dutch oven or heavy stovetop-to-oven casserole over medium-high heat, heat the oil until hot but not smoking. Add the onions and cook until soft but not browned, 2 to 3 minutes. Remove the onions with a slotted spoon.

4. Add the meat to the hot oil and cook, turning once, until browned on both sides. Spoon the onions over the browned meat. Pour the tomatoes around the pieces of meat.

5. Cover the pan and bake in the oven until the meat is tender, 2½ to 3 hours.

Serving suggestion: Divide the pieces of meat among 4 to 6 serving plates. Spoon some of the sauce over each portion. Serve any remainder in a warmed sauceboat on the side. Good with Mom's Mashed Potatoes or Buttered Noodles.

★*A meat mallet is a hammer-like instrument with a spiky head made for pounding meat.*
Many versions are two-headed; the spiky side is for meats with tough connective tissues,

Simple Pot Roast with Gravy

This is good old-fashioned pot roast. My husband says it reminds him of the way his mother used to cook.

SERVES 6 TO 8

ROAST:
1 point-cut beef rump roast (3 to 4 pounds)
   (See Wooden Spoon Kitchen Wisdom: Pot Roast, page 12)
1 tablespoon Worcestershire sauce
1 teaspoon salt
¼ teaspoon pepper
1 tablespoon all-purpose flour
1 tablespoon extra-virgin olive oil
1½ cups boiling water

GRAVY:
3 tablespoons all-purpose flour
¼ cup cold water
salt and pepper

1. Preheat the oven to 200°F.

2. Prepare the roast: Rub the meat with the Worcestershire sauce. Sprinkle the meat on all sides with the salt and pepper. Coat the surface of the meat with the flour.

3. Heat the oil in a dutch oven or heavy stovetop-to-oven casserole over medium-high heat. Brown the meat on all sides in the hot oil. Add the boiling water.

4. Cover the pan and roast in the oven until the meat is tender, 2 to 2½ hours (it should still have a rosy hue in the center). Halfway

the smooth side for tenderer cuts like scallopini or chicken breasts. Lacking that efficient tool, use the side of a heavy nonbreakable plate or the butt end of a table knife to do your pounding.

through the cooking time, turn the meat over with 2 large spoons or with tongs; do not pierce with a fork. At the end of the cooking time, transfer the meat to a warm platter while preparing the gravy.

5. Prepare the gravy: Mix the flour with the cold water. Stir a little of the cooking liquid into the flour-water mixture to warm it. Stir the mixture into the cooking liquid. Cook over medium heat, stirring, until thickened, about 2 minutes. Taste and add salt and pepper to taste. Strain, if needed.

Serving suggestion: Carve the meat into thin slices and spoon some of the gravy over the slices. Serve the remaining gravy in a warmed sauceboat. Good with Mom's Mashed Potatoes or Brown Rice.

Wooden Spoon Kitchen Wisdom: Pot Roast

Beef for pot roast needs to have enough marbling (streaks of fat) to allow the meat to cook to tenderness under gentle moist heat conditions. My favorite cut is a 3- to 4-pound point-cut rump. This cut comes from the bottom round, toward the sirloin end. It is a triangular cut, squared at the end where it was separated from the rest of the bottom round, pointed at the end adjoining the sirloin. It is compact, moderately marbled, and easy to slice when cooked.

Watch that you don't overcook a pot roast with too high a temperature, or with too long a braising time. Either one can result in dry, stringy beef. As the roast cooks, the beef fibers shrink, literally squeezing the juices into the braising liquid. If your roast becomes dried out, slice it, and return the slices to the gravy just long enough to be heated through.

Sauerbraten

The beef for sauerbraten is tenderized by soaking it for several days in a spicy, acidic marinade. It is then braised in liquid until tender, and a gravy is made with the braising liquid.

SERVES 6 TO 8

MARINADE:

2 cups cool water

1 cup red wine vinegar

1 cup dry red wine

1 medium onion, thinly sliced

1 garlic clove, minced or pressed

2 bay leaves, broken

6 whole cloves

1 teaspoon black peppercorns

¼ cup firmly packed brown sugar

SAUERBRATEN AND GRAVY:

1 boneless top blade roast (3 pounds)

1 tablespoon extra-virgin olive oil

1 medium onion, chopped

beef broth, as needed

3 tablespoons all-purpose flour

⅓ cup cold water

1. Prepare the marinade: Combine all the ingredients in a nonreactive saucepan. Heat until hot, but not boiling.

2. Prepare the sauerbraten: Place the beef in a nonreactive bowl and pour the hot marinade over it. Cover and refrigerate for 2 to 4 days, turning the meat once a day.

3. Preheat the oven to 275°F. Remove the meat from the marinade and pat dry. Strain the marinade, reserving the liquid.

4. Heat the oil over medium-high heat in a dutch oven or stovetop-to-oven casserole. Add the chopped onion and cook, stirring, until tender, about 2 minutes. Remove with a slotted spoon and reserve. Add the meat to the pot and lightly brown all sides in the hot fat. Return the onions to the pot.

5. Make 2½ cups braising liquid by combining part of the reserved marinade with beef broth. (The proportions of this can vary from all marinade to all beef broth. I prefer about ½ cup marinade and 2 cups broth.) Pour the braising liquid over the meat. Heat to just under a simmer.

6. Cover the pot and roast in the hot oven until the meat is tender, 3 to 3½ hours. Turn the meat, bottom-side up, halfway through the cooking time, taking care not to pierce the meat. Remove the meat from the braising liquid and let rest while you make the gravy.

7. Prepare the gravy: Set the pot of braising liquid over medium heat on stovetop. Stir together the flour and cold water until smooth. Add the flour mixture to the braising liquid. Cook, stirring constantly, until thickened, 3 to 4 minutes.

Serving suggestion: Carve the meat across the grain into thin slices. Spoon some of the gravy over the meat. Serve any remaining gravy on the side in a warmed sauceboat. Good with Olive Oil Mashed Potatoes or Buttered Noodles.

Fruited Beef Brisket

It's intriguing how seemingly different ingredients can come together to form a whole that is quite different from any of its parts. The spice-braised beef and stewed fruit described here is such an example.

SERVES 6 TO 8

1 teaspoon extra-virgin olive oil
3½ pounds beef brisket
2 cups hot water
1 tablespoon mixed pickling spices
¾ teaspoon salt
1 tablespoon firmly packed light brown sugar
1 tablespoon cider vinegar
½ cup pitted prunes
½ cup dried apricots
½ cup dried currants

1. Preheat the oven to 275°F.

2. Heat the oil in a dutch oven or heavy stovetop-to-oven casserole over medium-high heat. Brown the meat on all sides, finishing up with the fat side down. Add the hot water, pickling spices, and salt. Cover the pot and roast in the oven for 2 hours.

3. Remove the pot from the oven; leave the oven on. Remove the beef from the pot, taking care not to pierce the meat. Strain the braising liquid into a heatproof bowl. Add the brown sugar, vinegar, and dried fruits to the liquid; stir to blend well.

4. Return the meat to the pot, fat side up. Pour the fruited liquid around the meat. Cover, return to the oven, and roast until the meat is tender, about 1 hour longer. Remove the meat to a serving platter.

Serving suggestion: Carve the meat into thin slices. Serve the fruited sauce in a bowl on the side. We like this with Orange-Fennel Rye Bread or Porch Supper Pan Rolls.

Wooden Spoon Kitchen Wisdom: About Beef Brisket

A brisket is a rather large, flat piece of beef that comes from the steer's underside, just behind the front leg. The same cut, when pickled, becomes corned beef.

Beef Bourguignonne

This is less involved than many classic recipes for Beef Bourguignonne. The results are great.

SERVES 6

2 tablespoons extra-virgin olive oil
1 medium onion, chopped
1 garlic clove, minced or pressed
1½ pounds beef sirloin or round, cut into 1-inch cubes
1 cup dry red wine
1 can (14 to 16 ounces) beef broth
2 bay leaves
1 teaspoon fresh thyme leaves or ½ teaspoon dried
1 teaspoon fresh marjoram leaves or ½ teaspoon dried
¼ teaspoon salt
¼ teaspoon pepper
4 large carrots, cut in a rolling cut*, or 1 pound peeled baby
    carrots
12 ounces button mushrooms, halved lengthwise
    (if they are small, leave them whole)
8 ounces pearl onions, peeled and left whole
3 tablespoons all-purpose flour
3 tablespoons unsalted butter, softened
2 slices bacon, crisp-cooked, drained, and crumbled
chopped fresh parsley

1. In a nonreactive 4- to 5-quart stockpot over medium heat, heat 1 tablespoon of the oil. Add the chopped onion and garlic and

cook, stirring often, until the onion is tender, about 2 minutes. Remove with a slotted spoon and reserve.

2. Add the remaining 1 tablespoon oil to the pot. Cook the cubes of meat in the oil, stirring often, until all sides are browned.

3. Return the onion and garlic to the pot, and add the wine, broth, bay leaves, thyme, marjoram, salt, and pepper; bring to a boil. Reduce the heat, cover, and simmer for 1 hour.

4. Add the carrots, mushrooms, and pearl onions. Cover and simmer until the carrots are tender, about 30 minutes.

5. Remove the bay leaves. Mash together the butter and flour and drop, bit by bit, into the simmering broth, stirring all the while. Stir in the bacon. Sprinkle the parsley on top.

Serving suggestion: Transfer the stew to a serving bowl before garnishing with the parsley. Serve with Long-Grain Rice or Buttered Noodles.

★Rolling cut: Cut the carrot at a slant. Roll the carrot a quarter turn and cut again at a slant. Continue in this fashion to produce 3-sided pieces.

Bacon-Beef Stew Pot

This is one of those meals that cooks while you're out having fun—and tastes like you've slaved all day.

SERVES 6

3 slices thick-sliced bacon, diced
2 pounds lean beef round, cut into 1-inch cubes
4 medium onions, thinly sliced
6 medium potatoes, peeled and thinly sliced
1 to 1½ teaspoons salt, depending on the saltiness of the bacon
¼ teaspoon pepper
2 tablespoons chopped fresh parsley
2 cups cold water

1. Preheat the oven to 300°F.

2. In a dutch oven, or heavy stovetop-to-oven casserole over medium heat, sauté the bacon until beginning to brown, but not yet crisp. Remove the bacon with a slotted spoon. Discard the rendered fat, or save for later use.

3. Add to the pot, layering the ingredients in this order: half of the meat, half of the onions, half of the potatoes, and half of the bacon; sprinkle with half of the salt and half of the pepper. Repeat the layering using the remaining ingredients. Sprinkle with the parsley. Pour in the water. Bring slowly to a simmer.

4. Cover the pot and stew in the hot oven until the meat and vegetables are very tender, 2½ to 3 hours.

Serving suggestion: Tossed Green Salad and Old-Fashioned Dinner Rolls make perfect accompaniments.

Braised Boneless Short Ribs of Beef

More and more these days, supermarkets stock meat that is prepackaged without bones. It's a pity, because the bones add flavor to the broth that can't be replaced by other means. After searching several supermarkets for "bone-in" short ribs and finding none, I decided that a recipe for what I could find would be more useful to you than one for something that was unavailable. If, however, you do find short ribs with the bones intact, you can substitute with plans to serve only four.

SERVES 6

¼ *teaspoon salt*
¼ *teaspoon pepper*
⅓ *cup all-purpose flour*
3 pounds boneless short ribs of beef, cut into 3-inch pieces
2 tablespoons extra-virgin olive oil
2 tablespoons unsalted butter
2 carrots, coarsely chopped

2 celery ribs, coarsely chopped
2 medium onions, coarsely chopped
1 can (14 to 16 ounces) beef broth
1 can (8 ounces) tomato sauce
pinch of dried thyme
1 bay leaf

1. Shake the salt, pepper, and flour together in a plastic sack to mix. Add the beef, 1 piece at a time, and shake to coat with the flour mixture.

2. Heat the oil and butter over medium-high heat in a dutch oven or heavy stovetop-to-oven casserole. Add the meat and brown on both sides; remove the pieces as they brown.

3. Add the carrots, celery, and onions to the pot and cook, stirring, until they are glazed and fragrant. Sprinkle the remaining seasoned flour over the vegetables and stir to mix. Add the broth, tomato sauce, thyme, and bay leaf. Cook, stirring, until the mixture reaches a gentle simmer. Return the meat to the pot, nestling the pieces in among the vegetables. Cover the pot and simmer gently until the meat is tender, 2 to 2½ hours. (Alternately cook in a preheated 275°F oven for the same length of time.)

4. Remove the bay leaf; skim off any floating fat.

Serving suggestion: Perfect with Polenta or Buttered Noodles.

Corned Beef and Cabbage with Potatoes

Some cooks boil cabbage and potatoes in the same pot as corned beef. That makes everything taste like corned beef. I prefer to cook them separately, so that the flavors of the cabbage and potatoes are fresh and clean for a nice complement to the beef.

SERVES 6 (WITH SOME CORNED BEEF LEFT OVER
FOR SANDWICHES OR HASH)

3 pounds corned beef brisket
1 garlic clove, minced or pressed
1 teaspoon black peppercorns
1 bay leaf
6 large red potatoes
1 medium head green cabbage, cored
boiling water

1. Prepare the corned beef: Place the corned beef in a large pot with the garlic, peppercorns, and bayleaf; add cold water to cover by 1 inch. Bring slowly to a boil. Reduce the heat, cover, and simmer until the beef is very tender, about 3 hours. Transfer to a platter and let sit for 10 to 15 minutes before serving.

2. Meanwhile, scrub the potatoes, but do not peel. Place in a large pot, cover with cold water, and bring slowly to a boil. Reduce the heat to medium-low, cover, and cook until the potatoes are fork-tender, about 30 minutes.

3. While the potatoes are cooking, wash the cabbage; cut into 6 wedges. Place in a large pot. Cover the cabbage with boiling water. Cover the pot and simmer over low heat until fork-tender, about 15 minutes.

Serving suggestion: Carve the corned beef into thin slices. Place 1 potato and 1 wedge of cabbage on each serving plate. Arrange several thin slices of corned beef overlapping one edge of the cabbage. Offer salt, pepper, and butter to dress the cabbage and the potatoes.

Country Meat Loaf

You can vary this meat loaf by using all beef or substituting veal or turkey for the pork. You can also choose different herbs for flavoring, if you wish.

SERVES 4 TO 6

1 pound lean ground beef
8 ounces lean ground pork
½ cup soft whole wheat bread crumbs
½ medium onion, finely chopped
⅓ cup finely chopped celery
¼ cup chopped fresh parsley
½ teaspoon chopped fresh rosemary leaves or a pinch of dried
¼ teaspoon fresh thyme leaves or a pinch of dried
1 teaspoon salt
1 large egg
1 can (8 ounces) tomato sauce
1 teaspoon light brown sugar
1 teaspoon red wine vinegar

1. Preheat the oven to 350°F.

2. In a large bowl, mix both meats with the bread crumbs, onion, celery, parsley, rosemary, thyme, salt, and egg. In a small bowl, mix the tomato sauce, brown sugar, and vinegar. Add ¼ cup of the tomato sauce mixture to the meat loaf mixture and mix well.

3. Lightly pack the meat loaf mixture into an 9×5-inch loaf pan; level the top. Place in the hot oven and bake for 40 minutes.

4. Remove the meat loaf from the oven; spread ¼ cup of the tomato sauce mixture over the top of the loaf. Return to the oven and bake until done, about 30 minutes longer.

Serving suggestion: Remove the meat loaf to a serving platter and cut into ½-inch slices. Serve the remaining tomato sauce mixture on the side. Good with Scalloped Potatoes.

Sausage Loaf

The sausage flavors and moistens this meat loaf, making it quick to put together.

SERVES 6 TO 8

1 pound ground round of beef
1 pound seasoned bulk pork sausage
1 medium onion, chopped
¾ cup soft bread crumbs
¼ cup chopped fresh parsley
½ teaspoon salt
⅛ teaspoon ground pepper
¼ cup milk
1 large egg

1. Preheat the oven to 350°F.

2. Mix the meats with all of the remaining ingredients.

3. Lightly pack the meat loaf mixture into a 9×5-inch loaf pan; level the top. Bake in the oven until the loaf pulls away from the sides of the pan and no pink juices flow when the loaf is sliced, about 1½ hours.

Serving suggestion: Remove the meat loaf to a serving platter and cut into ½-inch slices. We like this with Butter-Baked Potatoes.

Stuffed Cabbage

This ends up with a flavorful, but juicy sauce. Serve it in shallow soup plates with plenty of crusty bread for soaking up the juices, or give it an old-world presentation with mashed potatoes on the side.

SERVES 6

12 large green cabbage leaves
1 pound lean ground beef

1 cup cooked long-grain or brown rice
1 cup minced onion
1 large egg
1 teaspoon salt
¼ teaspoon pepper
1 tablespoon chopped fresh parsley
1 teaspoon fresh thyme leaves or ¼ teaspoon dried
1 teaspoon fresh rosemary leaves or ¼ teaspoon dried
2 cups chopped canned tomatoes
1 cup beef broth
2 tablespoons firmly packed light brown sugar
1 tablespoon cider vinegar

1. Preheat the oven to 350°F.

2. Drop the cabbage leaves into a large pot of boiling water and cook until softened, about 1 minute. Drain well.

3. In a large bowl, combine the ground beef, rice, ½ cup of the onion, the egg, salt, pepper, parsley, thyme, and rosemary. Divide the meat mixture into 12 equal portions. Place 1 portion on each cabbage leaf, fold in the sides of the cabbage to completely enclose the stuffing, and roll up. Place the rolls, seam sides down, in a large flat covered casserole.

4. In another bowl, stir together the tomatoes, broth, brown sugar, and vinegar; pour the mixture over the cabbage rolls.

5. Cover the casserole and bake until the stuffing mixture is cooked through, about 45 minutes.

Serving suggestion: Place the cabbage rolls in shallow soup plates and spoon some of the sauce into the bowl. If desired, serve a dollop of Olive Oil Mashed Potatoes to the side of the cabbage. Thick slices of A Peasant Loaf will help sop up the juices.

Stuffed Peppers

Use the stuffing recipe for Stuffed Cabbage (see above). Cut the tops off 6 green bell peppers. Remove the membranes and seeds. Stuff with the meat mixture. Prepare the sauce mixture from Stuffed Cabbage and pour around the peppers in a shallow casserole. Bake uncovered at 350°F until the stuffing mixture is done, about 45 minutes.

Gourmet Hamburgers

Simple enhancements can turn plain hamburger into gourmet fare. These are good with or without buns.

SERVES 2 TO 4

1 pound ground beef chuck
¼ cup finely chopped onion
1 tablespoon chopped fresh parsley
½ teaspoon salt
⅛ teaspoon pepper
1 tablespoon dry red wine

1. In a medium bowl, gently but thoroughly mix together all of the ingredients. Shape into 4 uniform patties, each about ⅜ inch thick.

2. In a large nonstick skillet over medium heat, panfry the patties, turning several times, until they reach desired doneness, 5 to 7 minutes for medium.

Serving suggestion: Serve on a plate surrounded by steamed or simmered green beans, carrots, and summer squash.

Open-Faced Hamburgers

I learned how to make these from my mother. They became one of the
six meals that I repeated week after week as a bride, until I decided I
really must learn how to cook. Although my husband tired of them
when we were first married, he tells me he rather relishes them when
they are not such a common occurrence.

SERVES 3 TO 6

1 pound ground beef chuck
½ teaspoon salt
¼ teaspoon pepper
3 tablespoons finely minced onion
3 tablespoons ketchup
1 medium egg (or the smallest egg in a dozen large)
6 slices bread

1. Preheat the oven to 350°F.

2. In a medium mixing bowl, combine the beef, salt, pepper,
onion, ketchup, and egg. Divide into 6 portions; spread each portion
over 1 slice of the bread.

3. Place the hamburgers on a baking sheet. Bake until browned,
about 25 minutes.

Serving suggestion: Perfect with Refrigerator Coleslaw and Black
Beans.

Sloppy Joes

Sloppy Joes are, well, sloppy. You can eat them open-faced, with a knife and fork, if you want to cut down on spills.

SERVES 6

1½ pounds ground beef round
1 medium onion, finely chopped
1 celery rib, finely chopped
½ green bell pepper, finely chopped
1 cup beef broth
1 cup chili sauce
1 tablespoon Worcestershire sauce
⅛ to ¼ teaspoon Tabasco sauce, according to your taste
salt and pepper

1. In a nonreactive medium saucepan over medium-high heat, cook the beef, onion, celery, and bell pepper, stirring often, until the meat is browned, 3 to 5 minutes.

2. Stir in the beef broth, chili sauce, Worcestershire, and Tabasco. Add salt and pepper to taste. Simmer, uncovered, stirring now and then, until thickened, 15 to 20 minutes.

Serving suggestion: Serve on toasted buns. Good with an assortment of raw vegetable sticks.

Family-Style Chili

This is a mild chili that's good to keep on hand when the cold winds blow.

SERVES 4

1 pound lean ground beef
1 medium onion, chopped

1 garlic clove, minced or pressed
1 tablespoon chili powder
¾ teaspoon salt
1 teaspoon cornmeal
½ teaspoon ground cumin
1 can (14 to 16 ounces) tomatoes, with their juices, crushed
1 can (14 to 16 ounces) light red kidney beans, drained
1 can (8 ounces) tomato sauce

1. In a nonreactive medium saucepan over medium heat, cook the beef, onion, and garlic, stirring now and then, until the meat loses all pink color, about 3 minutes.

2. Stir together the chili powder, salt, cornmeal, and cumin; stir into the meat mixture. Add the tomatoes and their juices, beans, and tomato sauce. Reduce the heat and simmer, uncovered, stirring now and then, for 15 to 20 minutes.

Serving suggestion: Serve in heavy pottery bowls. Good with Pick-Your-Color Corn Bread.

Veal Scallopini

I don't always find thin slices of veal, or scallopini, in the meat case. When that happens I substitute with a small boneless veal roast, slicing thin pieces across the grain of the meat with a sharp knife.

SERVES 4

¼ cup all-purpose flour
¼ teaspoon salt
¼ teaspoon white pepper
1 pound veal scallopini
about 1 tablespoon extra-virgin olive oil
about 1 tablespoon unsalted butter
½ cup dry white wine

1. Preheat the oven to 200°F.

2. On a piece of waxed paper, stir together the flour, salt, and pepper. Coat the pieces of the veal lightly with the flour mixture and lay them out on additional waxed paper.

3. In a nonstick skillet, heat the oil and butter over medium-high heat. Brown the scallopini on both sides in the oil-butter mixture, taking care not to crowd the skillet. Remove them to a platter as they brown and keep them warm in the oven.

4. When all of the veal is browned, add the wine to the skillet. Boil, scraping the bottom of the pan and stirring constantly, until the wine is reduced by half.

Serving suggestion: Pour the reduced wine over the scallopini and serve immediately. Good with Lentils and Long-Grain Rice.

Veal Birds

Veal birds are simply slices of veal rolled around a bread-crumb filling, sautéed in butter, and sauced with a splash of white wine. They are supposed to resemble tiny stuffed birds.

SERVES 4

8 boneless veal cutlets, cut about ¼ inch thick
 (about 1 pound total weight)
6 tablespoons (¾ stick) unsalted butter
1 small onion, finely chopped
1 cup soft bread crumbs
1 teaspoon chopped fresh marjoram or ¼ teaspoon dried
⅛ teaspoon salt
pinch of pepper
3 tablespoons all-purpose flour
⅔ cup dry white wine

1. With the flat side of a meat mallet or the butt end of a table knife, pound each piece of veal until slightly flattened.

2. In a nonreactive large skillet over medium-high heat, melt 2 tablespoons of the butter. Add the onion and cook, stirring often, until tender, 2 to 3 minutes. Stir in the bread crumbs, marjoram, salt, and pepper. Remove from the heat.

3. Divide the mixture evenly among the veal cutlets, patting the stuffing evenly into place. Roll up from a short side, jelly-roll fashion; secure with round toothpicks; roll the veal birds in just enough of the flour to coat lightly.

4. Heat the remaining 4 tablespoons butter in the skillet over medium-high heat. Add the veal birds and cook, turning to cook all sides, until no pink remains. They need only brown very lightly. Remove the birds as they brown.

5. Add the remaining flour to the butter in the skillet and cook, stirring, to loosen any browned bits that cling to the bottom. Pour in the wine all at once. Cook, stirring constantly, until thickened. Remove from the heat.

6. Return the veal birds to the skillet. Set over medium-low heat, cover, and simmer until the veal is fork-tender, about 30 minutes.

Serving suggestion: Arrange the veal birds on serving plates; remove the toothpicks. Pour the wine sauce over the veal. Serve with Wild Rice or Buttered Noodles.

Veal Stew

Everything in this stew is light in flavor, so as not to overwhelm the delicate veal.

SERVES 4

2 tablespoons unsalted butter
1 tablespoon extra-light olive oil
1 pound cubed veal, trimmed of excess fat
8 ounces pearl onions, peeled and left whole
2 carrots, sliced
3 tablespoons all-purpose flour
about 1 cup chicken broth
⅓ cup dry white wine
salt and white pepper
chopped fresh parsley, for garnish

1. In a nonreactive medium saucepan, melt the butter in the oil over medium-high heat. Add the veal in batches and cook on all sides until no pink color remains; remove the pieces of the veal as they cook. (They don't need to brown.)

2. Add the onions and carrots to the pan. Cook, stirring, to glaze them, about 2 minutes. Sprinkle the flour over the vegetables and stir to coat the vegetables evenly with the flour. Pour the broth into the pan and bring almost to a boil. Cook, stirring, until thickened.

3. Return the veal to the pan; stir in the wine. Add additional broth, if needed, to thin the stew. Don't be hasty, however, as the veal will provide some juices to the mix. Cover the pan and simmer gently until tender, 1 to 1½ hours. Add salt and pepper to taste. Garnish with the parsley.

Serving suggestion: Excellent with Polenta or Buttered Noodles.

Wooden Spoon Kitchen Wisdom:
Prevention of Trichinosis in Eating Pork

The proper cooking of pork to an internal temperature of 137°F will destroy trichinosis organisms, and the most often cited temperature range for cooked pork is 160° to 170° to ensure safety while preserving optimum juiciness and flavor. Although some chefs prepare pork to a more rare temperature, citing the low incidence of infestation, I prefer to cook my pork to the recommended range for safety. Why take chances with a painful disease that could be life threatening?

A second method of prevention of trichinosis is to freeze pork at a temperature below 5° for a minimum of twenty days. If you wish to rely on this method, be sure your freezer can maintain the temperature you need. (Source: *Trichinosis: Risk and Prevention*, by Rom Carr, Ph.D. Facts from the Meat Board Series, National Livestock and Meat Board, 1992.)

Roast Loin of Pork with Pan Gravy

Starting this roast at a high temperature provides you with a crackling-crisp crust, succulent pork, and proper drippings to produce a rich, brown gravy.

SERVES 8

1 bone-in pork loin roast (about 4 pounds)
salt and pepper
1 cup hot water
2 tablespoons all-purpose flour
¼ cup cold water

1. Preheat the oven to 450°F.

2. Sprinkle the roast on all sides with salt and pepper. Place in a shallow roasting pan without a rack, bone-side down. Roast for 20 minutes.

31

3. Reduce the oven temperature to 350°. Continue roasting until a meat thermometer inserted in the center of the roast, away from the bone, registers 160° to 170°, about 2 hours longer (30 minutes per pound). Transfer to a serving platter and let stand while making the gravy.

4. Spoon off the fat from the roasting pan. Add the hot water to the pan and cook over medium heat, stirring to loosen any browned bits that stick to the bottom. Stir the flour into the cold water; stir into the pan. Cook, stirring, until thickened, 2 to 4 minutes. Add salt and pepper to taste.

Serving suggestion: Carve the meat into thin slices. Spoon a little of the gravy over the meat. Serve any remaining gravy in a warmed sauceboat. Good with Mom's Mashed Potatoes.

Roast Pork with Sweet-Sour Sauce

Pork is particularly suited to sweet and sour saucing. Leftovers can be sliced or cubed to be reheated in whatever sauce remains.

SERVES 6

ROAST:

3 pounds boneless pork loin
1 tablespoon soy sauce
1 garlic clove, cut into slivers

SAUCE:

1 cup firmly packed light brown sugar
1 cup cider vinegar
½ cup dry sherry
1 tablespoon soy sauce
½ teaspoon ground ginger
2 tablespoons cornstarch
¼ cup cool water

1. Preheat the oven to 450°F.

2. Prepare the roast: Rub the pork all over with the 1 tablespoon soy sauce. Place the roast, fat-side up, fitted on a rack in a roasting pan. Cut slits in the fat and insert the slivers of garlic. Place in the oven and immediately reduce the temperature to 350°. Roast until a meat thermometer inserted in the center registers 160° to 170°, about 1½ hours. Remove from the oven and let stand while preparing the sauce.

3. Prepare the sauce: In a nonreactive medium saucepan, stir together the brown sugar, vinegar, sherry, soy sauce, and ginger. Skim the fat from the roasting pan and discard; pour any remaining drippings into the sauce. Cook over medium-high heat, stirring now and then, until simmering. Stir together the cornstarch and cool water; stir into the sauce. Continue to cook, stirring constantly, until smooth and thickened, 1 to 2 minutes.

Serving suggestion: Serve slices of the pork with Brown Rice. Spoon the sauce over all.

Stuffed Pork Chops with Milk Gravy

I use homemade bread for the stuffing in these pork chops, but any good-quality bread will do. The vegetable-studded stuffing in the center of the chops with the old-fashioned milk gravy spooned over the top makes for mighty fine eating.

SERVES 4

PORK CHOPS:
4 pork chops, cut 1 inch thick
1 cup soft bread crumbs
¼ cup finely chopped celery
¼ cup finely chopped onion
1 tablespoon finely chopped parsley
¼ teaspoon salt
1 tablespoon unsalted butter, melted
1 cup chicken broth

GRAVY:
1 cup milk
2 tablespoons cornstarch
salt and pepper

1. Preheat the oven to 350°F.

2. Prepare the pork chops: Starting from the edge away from the bone, cut a deep, wide pocket in each chop. Mix together the bread crumbs, celery, onion, parsley, and salt. Add the melted butter and 3 tablespoons of the broth to moisten. Stuff the pork chops with the mixture. Skewer the openings shut with round toothpicks. Place in a stovetop-to-oven baking dish large enough to hold the chops in a single layer without crowding. Pour the remaining broth around the chops.

3. Cover the casserole and bake until the chops are fork-tender and no pink is visible when cut, 45 to 60 minutes. Remove the chops to a serving platter. Remove the toothpicks from the chops.

4. Prepare the gravy: Stir together the milk and the cornstarch; stir into the broth in the casserole. Cook over medium-high heat, stirring, until thickened, 3 to 5 minutes. Add salt and pepper to taste. Strain the gravy, if needed, to remove any lumps.

Serving suggestion: Spoon a little gravy over the chops and serve the remainder in a warmed sauceboat on the side.

Oven–Barbecued Ribs with Homemade Barbecue Sauce

I prefer country-style ribs for this dish and the one that follows, because there is a greater ratio of meat to bones and fat.

SERVES 4

2½ to 3 pounds country-style pork ribs
1 teaspoon extra-virgin olive oil
1 medium onion, finely chopped
1 cup ketchup
⅓ cup firmly packed light brown sugar
¼ cup cider vinegar
1 tablespoon fresh lemon juice
¼ teaspoon pepper
¼ teaspoon crushed red pepper flakes
¼ teaspoon Tabasco sauce

1. Preheat the oven to 350°F.

2. Arrange the ribs in a 13×9-inch baking pan. Roast in the oven for 45 minutes.

3. While the ribs are roasting, prepare the sauce: In a medium saucepan, heat the oil over medium-high heat. Add the onion and cook, stirring, until tender, 2 to 3 minutes. Stir in all of the remaining ingredients. Reduce the heat to a simmer, and cook, stirring often, until slightly thickened, about 15 minutes.

4. Remove the ribs from the oven; pour off any accumulated fat. Slather the sauce all over the ribs. Return to the oven and roast until the ribs are glazed with the sauce and no pink shows when the meat is cut into, about 30 minutes longer. Baste the ribs every 15 minutes with additional sauce until all is used. Serve immediately.

Serving suggestion: Serve directly from the roasting pan. Good with Pineapple Slaw and Cream Biscuits.

Ribs and Sauerkraut

This is old-fashioned good eating that never goes out of style.

SERVES 4

2 pounds fresh-packed sauerkraut, rinsed and drained
   (look for this in the case where packaged meats are displayed)
2 medium onions, chopped
2 medium Granny Smith apples, peeled, cored, and diced
1 tablespoon packed light brown sugar
½ teaspoon caraway seeds
¼ teaspoon pepper
¼ cup dry white wine
1 bay leaf, broken in half
2½ to 3 pounds country-style pork ribs
salt and pepper

1. Preheat the oven to 325°F.

2. In a 13×9-inch baking dish or nonreactive pan, combine the sauerkraut, onions, apples, brown sugar, caraway seeds, and pepper. Spread evenly in the dish. Pour the wine evenly over the sauerkraut mixture. Poke a half bay leaf into 2 places in the mixture. Sprinkle the ribs lightly with salt and pepper. Arrange the ribs in single layer over the sauerkraut mixture. Tightly cover the dish with foil.

3. Bake in the oven until no pink shows when the ribs are cut into, about 1½ hours. Remove the bay leaf halves before serving.

Serving suggestion: Serve directly from the baking dish or pan. Good with slices of Orange-Fennel Rye Bread spread with softened sweet butter.

Baked Glazed Ham

I like to bake a ham that's large enough to afford some leftovers. Besides making the best of sandwiches or using the remainders in the recipes that follow, there are many ways that leftover ham can be used. Chopped ham can be added to a pot of cabbage or green beans, slivered ham goes well with honeydew melon in a salad, and ground ham makes an omelet special.

SERVES 12 TO 16

1 bone-in ham (about 10 pounds)
⅓ cup firmly packed light brown sugar
1 teaspoon dry mustard
1 tablespoon cider vinegar

1. Preheat the oven to 350°F.

2. Loosen the skin of the ham with a sharp knife and remove, leaving a small collar of skin around the shank end. Trim off all but a thin layer of the fat. Bake the ham until a meat thermometer inserted in the center registers 160°, 3¼ to 3½ hours or about 20 minutes per pound.

3. In a bowl, mix together the brown sugar, mustard, and vinegar to make the glaze.

4. One hour before the ham is done or when the meat thermometer registers 130°, remove the ham from the oven. Score the fat in a diamond pattern, cutting the surface of the meat ¼ inch deep. Brush with the glaze. Return to the oven and finish baking.

Serving suggestion: Carve the ham into thin slices and arrange on a serving platter. Good with Southern Green Beans and Home-Fried Potatoes.

Wooden Spoon Kitchen Wisdom: Cooking with Ham

When cooking with leftover ham, use a light hand with any seasonings, especially salt. The ham itself may be quite salty.

Ham and Cheese Soufflé

A soufflé is simply a white sauce thickened with egg yolks and lightened by beaten egg whites. The mixture transforms in the oven, rising right out of the dish as the trapped air from the beaten egg whites expands in the heat of the oven.

SERVES 4 TO 6

3 tablespoons unsalted butter
3 tablespoons all-purpose flour
1 cup milk, heated to hot
4 large eggs, separated
¼ teaspoon salt
1 teaspoon dry mustard
1 cup ground cooked ham
1 cup grated sharp cheddar cheese (about 4 ounces)

1. Preheat the oven to 375°F. Butter the bottom of a 2-quart soufflé dish; do not butter the sides.

2. In a nonreactive medium saucepan, melt the butter over medium heat. Add the flour and cook, stirring, for 2 minutes. Remove from heat. Quickly add the hot milk, stirring all the while. Return the pan to the heat and cook, stirring constantly, until thickened, 1 to 2 minutes. Remove from the heat.

3. Beat the egg yolks just until smooth. Mix a little of the white sauce into the yolks to warm them; stir the mixture into the saucepan. Return to medium heat and cook, stirring constantly, until thickened a

little bit more, about 1 minute. Remove from the heat. Stir in the salt, mustard, ham, and cheese. Stir gently just until the cheese begins to melt.

4. In a clean bowl, beat the egg whites until almost stiff. Stir one-fourth of the egg whites into the ham mixture to lighten it. Gently fold in the remaining egg whites. Spoon the mixture into the soufflé dish.

5. Bake in the oven until the top is puffed and browned and the soufflé is set, 35 to 45 minutes.

Serving suggestion: Serve at the table so diners can admire the height of the soufflé before the first spoonful deflates its glory. Asparagus with Buttered Crumbs is good with this soufflé.

Honey–Glazed Ham Loaf

This is delicious hot, and the leftovers are good sliced cold for lunch. If you don't have a food processor or meat grinder, have the butcher grind the ham and pork to the texture of ground beef.

SERVES 6 TO 8

1 pound lean baked ham
12 ounces lean pork
1 cup fresh bread crumbs
1 small onion, finely chopped
1 tablespoon chopped fresh parsley
¼ teaspoon salt
⅛ teaspoon pepper
¾ cup milk
2 large eggs, lightly beaten
¼ cup honey
1 teaspoon prepared mustard
1 tablespoon fresh lemon juice

1. Preheat the oven to 350°F.

2. Cut the ham and pork into chunks and process in a food processor or meat grinder until ground to the texture of ground beef. Mix the meats with the bread crumbs, onion, parsley, salt, and pepper. Add the milk and eggs and mix lightly. Lightly pack the mixture into a 9×5-inch loaf pan.

3. Mix together the honey, mustard, and lemon juice to make a glaze. Brush the top of the loaf with the glaze.

4. Bake the ham loaf until the loaf is done and the top is browned, about 1¾ hours. Let stand for 20 minutes before turning out on a platter to serve.

Serving suggestion: Cover the ham loaf with a platter and invert; cover with a second platter and invert again so that the glazed side is up. Carve into ¼-inch slices. Good with Scalloped Potatoes.

Ham and Potato Pancakes

This is a good way to stretch a little bit of leftover ham into a lunch for four.

SERVES 4

1 cup ground cooked ham (grind in a food processor)
1 cup leftover seasoned mashed potatoes
1 teaspoon minced fresh parsley
1 teaspoon minced onion
¼ teaspoon salt
pinch of pepper
2 large eggs, beaten
about 4 tablespoons (½ stick) unsalted butter

1. Mix together the ham and potatoes. Stir in the parsley, onion, salt, and pepper. Stir in the beaten eggs and mix until smooth.

2. Melt 1 tablespoon of the butter in a nonstick skillet. Drop the ham-potato mixture into the melted butter by heaping tablespoonfuls. Do not crowd the pan. Cook, turning once, until crisp and browned on both sides.

3. Add additional butter to the skillet as needed to cook the remaining pancakes. Serve hot from the skillet, or keep warm in the oven while the others are being cooked.

Serving suggestion: Transfer to plates. Good with Sautéed Apples or Fruity Waldorf.

Ham and Beans

After you have enjoyed most of your ham, you should be left with meaty bones—perfect for flavoring a pot of beans.

SERVES 6 TO 8

1 pound dried navy or pea beans
6 cups cold water, for soaking
1 tablespoon extra-virgin olive oil
2 onions, finely chopped
1 carrot, finely diced
2 garlic cloves, minced
6 cups cold water, for cooking
1 bay leaf
1 meaty ham bone from 1 baked ham
salt and pepper

1. Wash the beans and pick over to remove any dirt or pebbles. Place in a large stockpot and cover with the soaking water. Let stand for 6 to 8 hours, or overnight. Drain the beans; rinse the beans and drain again. Rinse and dry the stockpot.

2. Heat the oil in the pot over medium-high heat. Add the onions, carrot, and garlic and cook, stirring often, until the onions are

tender, 2 to 3 minutes. Add the drained beans, the cooking water, and the bay leaf. Slowly bring to a full boil. Reduce the heat to a simmer, cover, and cook for 1 hour.

3. Add the ham bone to the pot. Cover and simmer until the beans are very tender, 1 to 2 hours longer. Add water if the beans threaten to dry out.

4. Remove the bay leaf and discard. Remove the ham bone. Cut the meat from the bone. Chop the meat into bite-size pieces, and return the meat to the pot of beans. Add salt and pepper to taste.

Serving suggestion: Serve in heavy pottery bowls with Pick-Your-Color Corn Bread or on a plate with Polenta.

Wooden Spoon Kitchen Wisdom: Soaking Beans

If you forget to soak beans ahead of time, bring them to a boil in the soaking water and boil for 2 minutes. Remove from the heat and let the beans stand for 1 hour. Drain, cover with water, and cook as directed. To cut the time even more, boil the beans for 5 minutes, and soak for just 30 minutes before draining.

Don't add any salt or acids (such as tomato juice) to beans before they are thoroughly cooked, as these ingredients can prevent the beans from becoming tender.

Roast Leg of Lamb with Pan Gravy

The old-fashioned way to cook lamb is well-done. Modern cooks tend toward rare to medium-rare. Although I enjoy my lamb medium-rare, I sometimes cook it to medium-well; at this stage the meat is still succulent and the drippings for gravy are more plentiful.

SERVES 6

1 leg of lamb (5 to 6 pounds)
2 garlic cloves, cut into slivers
salt and pepper
1 cup hot water
1 can (14 to 16 ounces) beef broth (water can be substituted if
    the drippings are rich and plentiful)
3 tablespoons cornstarch
¼ cup cold water

1. Preheat the oven to 450°F.

2. If your leg of lamb has not been trimmed, you will need to remove any excess fat, leaving a thin layer next to the skin. Attach any flaps of meat to the body of the leg with toothpicks. Place the lamb, fat-side up, on a rack in a roasting pan. Cut slits in the top of the lamb, and insert the slivers of garlic. Sprinkle all over with salt and pepper.

3. Place the lamb in the oven and immediately reduce the heat to 350°. Roast until a meat thermometer inserted in the center but away from the bone registers 140° for rare, 145° for medium-rare, or 150° for medium, 1 to 1½ hours. If you want your lamb well-done, continue cooking it until the temperature reaches 160° to 175°. Remove the lamb to a platter and let stand while you prepare the gravy.

4. Spoon off the fat from the roasting pan, leaving the drippings. Stir in the hot water and scrape up any bits that stick to the bottom of the pan. Transfer to a medium saucepan. Add the beef broth, and bring to a simmer over medium heat. Stir together the cornstarch and cold water; stir into the gravy. Cook, stirring, until thickened, 1 to 2 minutes. Add salt and pepper to taste.

Serving suggestion: Carve the lamb into thin slices; fan out 3 or 4 slices on each plate; spoon a little of the gravy over the slices and serve the remainder in a warmed sauceboat on the side. We like this with Olive Oil Mashed Potatoes.

Marinated Leg of Lamb

This recipe uses equal parts of mustard, soy sauce, lemon juice, and olive oil to produce a piquant marinade that escapes being too mustardy or salty.

SERVES 8

1 leg of lamb (7 to 8 pounds)
2 garlic cloves, minced or pressed
2 tablespoons Dijon mustard
2 tablespoons soy sauce
2 tablespoons fresh lemon juice
2 tablespoons extra-virgin olive oil
1 tablespoon fresh rosemary leaves or 1 teaspoon dried

1. If your leg of lamb has not been trimmed, you will need to remove any excess fat, leaving a thin layer next to the skin. Attach any flaps of meat to the body of the leg with toothpicks. Place the lamb, fat side down, on a large sheet of foil.

2. In a small bowl, whisk together all of the remaining ingredients until smooth. Brush the exposed parts of the lamb with the marinade. Let stand at room temperature for 30 minutes.

3. Meanwhile, preheat the oven to 450°F.

4. Invert the leg, fat-side up, in a roasting pan. Score the fat in a crisscross pattern just deep enough to reach the meat. Brush the exposed parts with the marinade. Roast for 15 minutes.

5. Reduce the oven heat to 350° and roast until a meat thermometer inserted in the center of the roast away from the bone registers 140° for rare, 145° for medium-rare, or 150° for medium, 1½ to 2 hours longer. If you want your lamb well-done, continue cooking it until the temperature reaches 160° to 175°.

Serving suggestion: Carve the lamb into thin slices; fan out 3 or 4 slices on each plate. Good with Roasted Sweet and White Potato Sticks or Noodle-Rice Pilaf.

Roast Rack of Lamb

Rack of lamb is an elegant entrée that's easy to prepare. Have your butcher crack the chine bone between each rib, so that the rack will be easy to carve and serve.

SERVES 4

2 tablespoons Dijon mustard
2 tablespoons dry white wine
2 racks of lamb (each 6 to 8 ribs and 1½ to 2 pounds)
½ cup fresh bread crumbs
1 teaspoon fresh rosemary leaves or ½ teaspoon dried
2 tablespoons melted butter

1. Preheat the oven to 500°F.

2. Mix together the mustard and wine to make a smooth paste. Paint the mixture over the top and sides of the racks of lamb. Lightly press the bread crumbs into the mustard paste. Sprinkle with the rosemary. Drizzle the butter over all. Place the racks, meaty sides up, on a rack in a roasting pan.

3. Place in the oven and reduce the oven temperature to 400°. Roast until a meat thermometer inserted in the thickest part of the meat, away from the bone, registers 145° to 150°, about 30 minutes. If you want well-done lamb, continue cooking until the thermometer registers 165° to 170°. Let stand for 5 to 10 minutes before carving.

Serving suggestion: Carve the rack of lamb into double ribs to serve. Serve with Risotto or New Potatoes with Dill.

Rack of Lamb with Pesto

This is even easier than the mustard version. If you have no basil to make your own pesto, you can substitute store-bought.

SERVES 4

¼ cup Pesto (page 139)
2 racks of lamb (each 6 to 8 ribs and 1½ to 2 pounds)
½ cup fresh bread crumbs

1. Preheat the oven to 500°F.

2. Spread the pesto over the tops and sides of the racks of lamb. Gently press the bread crumbs into the pesto. Place the racks, meaty sides up, on a rack in a roasting pan.

3. Place in the oven and reduce the oven temperature to 400°. Roast until a meat thermometer inserted in the thickest part of the meat, away from the bone, registers 145° to 150°, about 30 minutes. If you want well-done lamb, continue cooking until the thermometer reaches 165° to 170°. Let stand for 5 to 10 minutes before carving.

Serving suggestion: Carve the rack of lamb into double ribs to serve. Good with Risotto or Polenta.

Braised Lamb Shanks

Though lamb shanks can be very tasty, they are mostly bone. You will need to allow one shank (about 1 pound) per person.

SERVES 4

1 teaspoon extra-virgin olive oil
4 lamb shanks
1 medium onion, chopped
1 garlic clove, minced or pressed

1 can (14 to 16 ounces) beef broth
½ cup dry red wine
grated zest of 1 lemon
⅛ teaspoon pepper
1 bay leaf
2 carrots, diced
2 celery ribs, diced
1 small turnip, peeled and diced
2 tablespoons all-purpose flour
2 tablespoons unsalted butter
salt and pepper

1. In a nonreactive heavy stockpot large enough to accommodate the shanks, heat the oil over medium–high heat. Add the shanks and brown on all sides. Remove the shanks with tongs and reserve.

2. Add the onion and garlic to the pot and cook, stirring, until the onion wilts, 2 to 3 minutes. Add the broth, wine, lemon zest, pepper, and bay leaf. Return the shanks to the pot; bring the liquids to a boil. Reduce the heat, cover, and simmer for 1 hour.

3. Remove the bay leaf. Add the carrots, celery, and turnip. Cover and simmer, stirring now and then, until the shanks and vegetables are tender, about 30 minutes longer. Remove the shanks to a serving platter; tent with foil to keep warm.

4. Skim off the fat from the broth and discard. Mash the butter and flour together and drop, bit by bit, into the simmering liquid, stirring all the while, until the mixture thickens. Add salt and pepper to taste.

Serving suggestion: Place each shank in a large flat bowl. Pour the vegetable gravy over and around the shanks. Serve with Pesto-Filled Rolls.

Leftover Lamb Ragout

If you roast a large leg of lamb, you will have leftovers for easy, tasty, follow-up meals like this.

SERVES 4

3 cups cubed cooked lamb
1 can (14 to 16 ounces) beef broth
2 medium carrots, cut into chunks
2 medium potatoes, cut into chunks
1 medium onion, coarsely chopped
1 bay leaf
¼ teaspoon fresh thyme leaves or a pinch of dried
1 tablespoon cornstarch
2 tablespoons cold water
salt and pepper
chopped fresh parsley, for garnish

1. In a medium saucepan, combine the lamb, broth, carrots, potatoes, onion, bay leaf, and thyme. Cover and simmer until the vegetables are tender, about 30 minutes. Remove the bay leaf.

2. Stir together the cornstarch and cold water. Stir into the pot, and cook, stirring, until thickened, 1 to 2 minutes. Add salt and pepper to taste.

Serving suggestion: Serve in flat bowls, garnished with the parsley. Good with Square Soda Biscuits or Porch Supper Pan Rolls.

Light Lamb Curry

This is a nice, light curry that combines leftover lamb with the sunshine flavors of lemon and golden raisins.

SERVES 4

2 tablespoons extra-light olive oil
2 onions, sliced
3 tablespoons all-purpose flour
1 teaspoon curry powder
1 can (14 to 16 ounces) chicken broth
1 tablespoon fresh lemon juice
3 tablespoons golden raisins
3 cups cubed cooked lamb

1. In a medium saucepan, heat the oil over medium heat. Add the onions and cook, stirring now and then, until the onions are tender, about 3 minutes. Sprinkle the flour and curry powder over the onions and stir. Add the chicken broth and cook, stirring, until the mixture thickens, 1 to 2 minutes.

2. Add the lemon juice, raisins, and lamb. Cover and simmer until the meat is heated through, 5 to 10 minutes.

Serving suggestion: Serve with Long-Grain Rice and Tomato-Apple or Peach Chutney.

Hash

Hash is a great dish that's made from leftovers, the raw materials of which are meat and potatoes that have already seen one life at a previous meal. The meats that can be used are roast beef, roast pork, roast lamb, baked ham, or cooked corned beef. The potatoes can be either white or red ones that have been boiled in their skins. The onion, bell pepper, and herbs are purely optional.

49

SERVES 4

2 tablespoons unsalted butter
2 cups cooked leftover meat, cubed
4 cooked leftover medium potatoes, peeled and cubed
1 tablespoon finely chopped onion (optional)
1 tablespoon finely chopped green bell pepper (optional)
a pinch or two of chopped fresh herbs, such as rosemary or thyme
    (optional)
salt and pepper

1. In large nonstick skillet, melt the butter over medium heat. Add the meat, potatoes, onion, bell pepper, and herbs and mix together. Cook, stirring now and then, until the potatoes are slightly crisp and browned and the meat is heated through and beginning to brown, 10 to 15 minutes. Add salt and pepper to taste. Serve hot.

Serving suggestion: Spoon onto plates in the kitchen. All you need with this is a Tossed Green Salad.

Meats That Fly

Most cookbooks provide one chapter called Meat and one called Poultry. I have never understood that nomenclature, because I consider poultry to be meat, just as much as beef, pork, and lamb are meats. Still wanting to divide the recipes into two parts, I renamed my meat chapters distinguishing between meat that flies and meat that doesn't. So here are my favorite recipes for geese, ducks, game hens, turkeys, and chickens.

Starting with a glorious goose stuffed with potatoes and splashed with celebratory Champagne, and going on to succulent roast duckling with orange sauce, brandy-basted game hens, traditional roast turkey, comforting country-fried chicken, old-fashioned chicken and noodles, here are those and many other favorites from a lifetime of cooking for my family.

Glorious Goose with Potato-Apple Stuffing and Champagne Gravy

The rich, dark meat of a goose is splendid fare, though not economical. An 8-pound bird, because it is so bony, will serve but 4 with some leftovers. Because of its extravagance, it seems only fitting to serve flutes of Champagne to add to the celebration. (Don't forget to reserve enough for the goose!)

The apples in the stuffing lend a tart balance to the richness of the goose, and since potatoes are included, take the opportunity to serve other vegetables with the meal. Something green and something red or orange would look nice on the plate. The splash of chilled Champagne near the end of the roasting time helps to crisp the skin, which, by then, should have given up much of its fat to the pan.

I've found that sometimes a goose's meat will be stringy. I don't know why, but if it happens to you, don't apologize.

SERVES 4

STUFFING:

4 medium potatoes (about 1 pound), peeled and diced

2 tablespoons butter

1 medium onion, chopped

1 celery rib, diced

2 tart apples, peeled, cored, and chopped

¼ teaspoon ground thyme

¼ teaspoon ground sage

1 tablespoon chopped fresh parsley

GOOSE:

1 goose (8 to 9 pounds), thawed if frozen

salt and pepper

¼ cup chilled Champagne

GRAVY:

about ½ cup giblet or chicken broth

¼ cup Champagne

2 tablespoons cornstarch

¼ cup cold water

salt and pepper

1. Prepare the stuffing: In a large saucepan, cover the potatoes with cold salted water. Bring to a boil over high heat. Reduce the heat to a simmer, cover, and cook just until tender, 10 to 15 minutes. Drain well.

2. Meanwhile, melt the butter in a small skillet over medium heat. Add the onion and celery and cook, stirring, until the onion is tender, 3 to 5 minutes.

3. In a large bowl, combine the onion mixture with the apples and potatoes and toss to mix. Add the thyme, sage, and parsley and toss again.

4. Preheat the oven to 450°F.

5. Prepare the goose: Use the giblets (not the liver) to make broth (page 56), or reserve for other use. Rinse the goose inside and out under cold, running water; drain well; pat dry with paper towels. Pull out any pieces of fat you find in the cavity and render for later use, if desired.

6. Loosely stuff the body cavity with the stuffing. With the breast facing you, lift the wings and bend behind the back of the bird. Tie the legs close to the body with kitchen string or white button and carpet thread. Place the goose on a rack in a shallow roasting pan; sprinkle all over with salt and pepper. Pierce the skin of the breast all over with a sharp fork or the tip of a knife, taking care not to pierce the meat.

7. Place the goose in the oven and immediately reduce the oven temperature to 350°. Roast until no pink juices appear when the thickest part of the thigh is pierced with a fork, 2¼ to 2¾ hours, or until a meat thermometer inserted in the thigh, away from the bone, registers 180° to 185°. Suction or spoon off the fat from the pan as it accumulates. During the last 10 minutes of roasting time, spoon the cold Champagne over the goose to crisp the skin. Remove the goose to a warm platter to rest while you make the gravy.

8. Prepare the gravy: Pour the drippings from the roasting pan into a large (4-cup) measuring cup and allow to settle. Remove the floating fat. Add enough broth to the remaining drippings to make 2 cups. Pour the Champagne into the roasting pan and simmer on stovetop over medium heat, stirring to loosen any browned bits that cling to the bottom of the pan. Add this mixture to the broth and drippings.

9. Strain the liquids into a nonreactive medium saucepan and bring to a simmer. Stir together the cornstarch and cold water. Add to the pot and cook, stirring, until thickened, about 2 minutes. Add salt and pepper to taste.

Serving suggestion: Carve the goose and arrange carved slices on a platter. Serve the gravy in a warmed sauceboat. Spoon the stuffing directly from the cavity of the bird. (Be sure to remove all of the stuffing from the bird before refrigerating leftovers.)

Wooden Spoon Kitchen Wisdom:
Rendering Goose or Duck Fat

Goose or duck fat can be rendered to use, in place of butter, for sautéing or flavoring potatoes or other vegetables. Chop the fat that you pull from the cavity of the bird. Cook with a small amount of water in a small saucepan over low heat until the fat is melted and the water has evaporated. Strain into a glass storage jar. Refrigerate to store. Keeps in the refrigerator for 1 month, in the freezer for 1 year.

The fat that accumulates in the roasting pan can also be saved, but it may not be as fine. I transfer the fat from a roasting goose into two small jars, rather than one large one. The first of the two contains the clearer fat.

Concentrated Giblet Broth

I like to make a concentrated broth by simmering the neck and giblets from fowl in chicken broth rather than water.

MAKES ABOUT 2 CUPS

> *neck and giblets from chicken, turkey, duck, or goose (not the*
> *liver)*
> *1 can (14 to 16 ounces) chicken broth*
> *½ bay leaf*

1. Rinse the neck and giblets under cold, running water. Score the neck between the bones, making cuts about 1 inch apart. (This makes removal of the meat after cooking a simple task.) Trim the heart and gizzard of any fat.

2. Place the parts in a large saucepan and add the chicken broth and bay leaf. Add water to cover, if needed. Bring slowly to a boil. Reduce the heat to a simmer, cover, and cook for 1½ to 2 hours.

3. Strain, reserving the broth and giblets separately. The meat from the neck, heart, and gizzard can be chopped to add to gravy or soup.

Wooden Spoon Kitchen Wisdom: Stuffing Poultry and Making Stuffings

Stuffings for poultry should be light in both texture and flavor. To avoid a soggy stuffing, prepare the mixture right before use and keep it fairly dry. It will absorb moisture from the bird as it cooks. The seasonings used should complement the flavor of the bird, not overpower it. Since the main ingredient of most stuffings is bread, the importance of a good-quality loaf is obvious. Mediocre bread will only result in a mediocre stuffing, no matter how fine the remaining ingredients may be.

The poultry's cavity should be stuffed loosely to allow for expansion during cooking and even penetration of heat throughout both the meat and the stuffing. Never stuff poultry more than a few minutes before roasting: Bacteria grow rapidly in raw poultry, and even a freshly made stuffing can spell disaster if stuffed into the bird ahead of time.

Roast Duckling with Orange Sauce

The first time I roasted a duckling, I prepared one five-pounder for my family of five. The children were small, and I expected them to opt for the hot dogs that were stockpiled in the refrigerator for meals that aroused their suspicions. They surprised me by taking more than expected, and I found myself supplementing with extra vegetables and bread.

The truth is that one duck serves 2 people well, with leftovers for lunch. There is enough meat for 3, but the carving does not work out well for more than 2 servings.

SERVES 2 TO 3

DUCK:

1 duck (4 to 5 pounds), thawed if frozen
½ lemon
salt and pepper
⅛ teaspoon ground thyme
⅛ teaspoon ground sage
1 small onion, peeled and quartered
1 small tart apple, peeled, cored, and quartered

ORANGE SAUCE:

1 cup giblet or chicken broth
½ cup fresh orange juice
2 tablespoons packed light brown sugar
grated zest of 1 navel orange
1 tablespoon cornstarch
2 tablespoons fresh lemon juice
2 tablespoons triple sec or curaçao (optional)
salt and pepper

1. Preheat the oven to 375°F.

2. Prepare the duck: Rinse the duck under cold running water; drain well; pat dry with paper towels. Rub the duck with the cut side of the lemon. Sprinkle inside and out with salt and pepper. Sprinkle the cavity with the thyme and sage. Place the onion and apple in the cavity. Use kitchen string or white button and carpet thread to tie the wings and legs close to the body of the bird. Pierce the skin of the duck all over with a sharp fork or the tip of a knife, taking care not to pierce the meat. Place on a rack in a shallow roasting pan.

3. Roast until no pink juices appear when the meatiest part of the thigh is pierced with a fork, about 2 hours, or until a meat thermometer inserted in the thigh, away from the bone, registers 180° to 185°. Suction or spoon away the fat as it accumulates in the roasting pan. Let the duck stand while you prepare the orange sauce.

4. Prepare the orange sauce: In a nonreactive small saucepan over medium heat, bring the broth, orange juice, brown sugar, and orange zest to a boil. Reduce the heat to a simmer and cook for 2 minutes. Stir together the cornstarch and lemon juice; add to the pan and cook, stirring, for 2 minutes. Remove from the heat. Stir in the triple sec. Add salt and pepper to taste. Serve warm.

Serving suggestion: Carve the duck and arrange on a serving platter. Spoon some orange sauce over the duck slices. Serve the remaining sauce in a warmed sauceboat on the side. Wild Rice is excellent with this.

Ducks Stuffed with Sauerkraut

This is an adaptation of a recipe given to me by caterer Jessie Boyd of Danville, Illinois. The combination of the sweet-sour stuffing and the rich, dark meat of the ducks is quite pleasing. The same stuffing could be used for a goose.

SERVES 4 (WITH LEFTOVERS)

*2 pounds fresh-packed sauerkraut (look for it where the
    packaged meats are displayed)*
1 medium onion, chopped
1 large Granny Smith apple, peeled, cored, and chopped
1¾ cups or 1 bottle (14 ounces) tangy-style ketchup
2 tablespoons packed light brown sugar
2 tablespoons caraway seeds
2 ducks (4½ pounds each), thawed if frozen
salt and pepper

1. Rinse and drain the sauerkraut. In a nonreactive large skillet, combine the sauerkraut, onion, apple, ketchup, brown sugar, and caraway seeds. Cook over medium–high heat, stirring often, until the onion is translucent and about half of the moisture has boiled away, 10 to 15 minutes.

2. Preheat the oven to 375°F.

3. Prepare the ducks: Rinse the ducks under cold, running water; drain well; pat dry with paper towels. Pierce the skin of the ducks all over with a sharp fork or the tip of a knife, taking care not to pierce the meat. Sprinkle inside and out with salt and pepper. Spoon the hot stuffing into the cavities of the ducks with a slotted spoon, leaving any excess moisture behind. Tie the wings and legs close to the birds with kitchen string or white button and carpet thread. Place on a rack in a shallow roasting pan.

4. Roast until no pink juices appear when the thickest part of the thigh is pierced with a fork, about 2 hours, or until a meat thermometer inserted in the thigh, away from the bone, registers 180° to 185°. Transfer to a warm platter.

Serving suggestion: Carve the ducks into serving pieces. Arrange a large spoonful of stuffing next to the duck on each plate. (Be sure to remove all of the stuffing from the bird before refrigerating any leftovers.)

Simple Cassoulet

This has an earthy richness that comes from the combination of slowly simmering beans with well-flavored sausage and duck. Other meats can be substituted or added. Cubed roasted lamb can take the place of part of the sausage. Meat from a roasted goose can substitute for the duck.

SERVES 8

1 pound pea or navy beans
6 cups cold water, for soaking
4 cups cold water, for cooking
2 tablespoons duck drippings or extra-virgin olive oil
1 garlic clove, minced
1 medium onion, chopped

1 *medium carrot, chopped*
1 *celery rib, chopped*
1 *whole onion, peeled and stuck with 4 cloves*
1 *bay leaf*
2 *tablespoons chopped fresh parsley*
1 *teaspoon fresh thyme leaves or ½ teaspoon dried*
1 *teaspoon salt*
1 *cup dry white wine*
1 *can (8 ounces) tomato sauce*
1 *pound pre-cooked Polish sausage*
1 *roasted duck (see Roast Duckling, page 57), the meat*
    removed from the bones and cut into bite-size pieces
freshly ground pepper
2 *slices bread, preferably homemade*
1 *tablespoon unsalted butter, softened*

1. Wash and pick over the beans, removing any stones and chaff. Combine the washed beans with the 6 cups soaking water in a large nonreactive stockpot and soak overnight. Drain; rinse the beans and drain again.

2. Rinse out the stockpot. Add the beans and the 4 cups cooking water. Slowly bring to a boil and boil for 2 minutes. Reduce the heat to a simmer, cover, and cook for 1 hour.

3. After the beans have cooked for 1 hour or so, heat the drippings in a skillet over medium heat. Add the garlic, chopped onion, carrot, and celery and cook, stirring often, until the onion is tender, 5 to 7 minutes.

4. Remove the vegetables with a slotted spoon and add to the beans. Add the whole onion stuck with cloves, the bay leaf, parsley, thyme, salt, wine, and tomato sauce to the pot. Cover and simmer until the beans are tender, about 1 hour. Remove the bay leaf and the onion stuck with cloves.

4. Preheat the oven to 300°F.

5. Cook the sausage in the skillet until browned on all sides. If the sausage is in hot dog-size links, leave whole; if not, cut into serving-size pieces.

6. In a large casserole, layer one-third of the bean mixture and half of the meats; sprinkle the layer with freshly ground pepper. Layer on half of the remaining beans, all of the remaining meats, and sprinkle with pepper. Top with the remaining beans. If there is not enough bean broth to cover the ingredients, add water.

7. Cover the casserole and bake for 1½ hours.

8. Meanwhile, spread the bread with the butter. Set on an oven rack or in a small toaster oven until lightly browned. Tear the toasted bread into chunks and process in a food processor to make coarse crumbs.

9. Sprinkle the crumbs over the top of the beans. Return the casserole to the oven and bake, uncovered, until the crumbs are browned, about 30 minutes longer.

Serving suggestion: Serve directly from the casserole. Good with Perfect Potato Bread or Cream Biscuits.

Brandy-Basted Game Hens

The brandy used in this recipe is Calvados, an apple brandy. I like to use V.S.O.P. that has been aged for about five years. You could use something less, but if you plan a small glass with coffee after the meal, you might as well buy the good stuff.

SERVES 4

4 Rock Cornish game hens (1¼ pounds each), thawed if
    frozen
1 small Granny Smith apple, peeled, cored, and quartered
4 onion slices
4 fresh parsley sprigs
4 tablespoons (½ stick) unsalted butter, melted

salt and pepper
½ cup apple jelly
½ cup Calvados

1. Preheat the oven to 375°F.

2. Remove the giblets from the hens and reserve for another use. Rinse the hens under cold running water; drain well and pat dry with paper towels. With the breast facing you, lift the wings and bend behind the backs of the birds. Place 1 piece of the apple, 1 onion slice, and 1 parsley sprig in each cavity. Tie the legs together. Place the hens in a baking dish large enough to accommodate them without crowding. Brush the hens with the melted butter. Sprinkle with salt and pepper.

3. Roast the hens for 25 minutes.

4. Meanwhile, heat the jelly in a nonreactive small saucepan over medium heat until it begins to melt. Add the Calvados and cook, stirring, until the jelly is completely melted. Remove from the heat and keep warm.

5. Baste the hens with the warm Calvados sauce. Continue to roast, basting every 5 to 10 minutes with the remaining sauce, until the juices run clear when one of the hens is tilted, 25 to 30 minutes longer. (Game hens are too small to accurately test with a meat thermometer.)

Serving suggestion: Place the hens on a warmed serving platter. Serve the tasty pan juices in a warmed sauceboat. Good with Fruited Rice Pilaf.

Game Hens with Port Wine Sauce

You can split game hens rather easily, since their bones are not as firm as those in other types of fowl. The roasted split halves are delicious finished with a coating of port wine sauce. If your hens are plump, you might get away with planning one-half bird per serving, but I would rather be blessed with leftovers than come up short.

SERVES 4

HENS:

4 Rock Cornish Game Hens (1¼ pounds each),
    thawed if frozen
4 tablespoons (½ stick) unsalted butter, melted
salt and pepper

SAUCE:

½ cup currant jelly
1 tablespoon unsalted butter
2 tablespoons fresh lemon juice
2 tablespoons cornstarch
1 cup port wine

1. Preheat the oven to 350°F.

2. Prepare the hens: Remove the giblets from the hens and re-serve for another use. Split the hens lengthwise, from head to tail. Rinse under cold, running water; drain well and pat dry with paper towels. Use about one-third of the melted butter to coat a shallow baking pan large enough to accommodate all 4 hens without crowding. Place the hen halves in the pan, skin sides up. Brush with the remaining melted butter. Sprinkle with salt and pepper.

3. Roast the hens in the oven for 45 minutes.

4. Meanwhile, prepare the sauce: In a nonreactive small sauce-pan over medium heat combine the jelly, butter, and lemon juice. Cook, stirring often, until the butter and jelly melt and the mixture is smooth. Stir the cornstarch into the port; stir into the sauce. Cook, stir-ring constantly, until the mixture thickens, about 2 minutes. Remove from the heat and keep warm.

5. Remove the hens from the oven and pour the sauce over them. Return to the oven and roast until no pink juices appear when the thickest part of the thigh is pierced with a fork, about 15 minutes longer.

Serving suggestion: Transfer the cooked hens to a warmed serving platter. Good with Long-Grain or Brown Rice.

Game Hens with Wild Rice Stuffing and Orange Marmalade Glaze

The combination of wild rice and currants makes an elegant stuffing for these hens. The orange glaze made with marmalade couldn't be easier.
SERVES 4

HENS:

4 Rock Cornish Game Hens (1¼ pounds each),
    thawed if frozen
3 tablespoons unsalted butter, melted
2 tablespoons finely chopped onion
1 cup cooked wild rice
¼ cup dried currants
pinch of ground thyme
pinch of ground sage
salt and pepper

GLAZE:

¾ cup orange marmalade
1 tablespoon dark rum
1 tablespoon unsalted butter

1. Preheat the oven to 375°F.

2. Prepare the hens: Remove the giblets from the hens and reserve for another use. Rinse the hens under cold running water; drain well and pat dry with paper towels. With the breast facing you, lift the wings and bend behind the backs of the birds.

3. In a small skillet over medium heat, heat 1 tablespoon of the butter. Add the onion and cook, stirring, until tender, 2 to 4 minutes. Remove from heat; stir in the rice, currants, thyme, and sage. Spoon one-fourth of the stuffing into each cavity. Tie the legs together. Place the hens in a baking dish large enough to accommodate all of them without crowding. Brush the hens with the remaining 2 tablespoons melted butter. Sprinkle with salt and pepper.

4. Roast the hens for 45 minutes.

5. Meanwhile, prepare the glaze: Heat the marmalade in a non-reactive small saucepan over medium heat until it begins to melt. Add the rum and butter and cook, stirring, until heated through. Remove from the heat and keep warm.

6. Baste the hens with the glaze. Return to the oven and roast until no pink juices appear when the thickest part of the thigh is pierced with a fork, 10 to 15 minutes longer. (Game hens are too small to accurately test with a meat thermometer.)

Serving suggestion: Transfer the hens to a warmed serving platter. Spoon any leftover glaze over the hens.

Roast Turkey with Currant-Pecan Stuffing and Giblet Gravy

I gave up defrosting frozen turkeys long ago, and opt for ordering a fresh one. This removes the chore of defrosting and frees my refrigerator space for other things. If you prefer frozen turkeys, be sure to follow the defrosting directions on the turkey package and allow ample time for the process. Otherwise, you will find yourself wrestling with a still partly frozen bird while the time for putting it in the oven looms near.

SERVES 18 TO 20

STUFFING:
8 tablespoons (1 stick) unsalted butter
1 medium onion, chopped
2 celery ribs, diced
8 cups lightly toasted bread cubes (I like to use Pepperidge
    Farm Toasting Bread, cubed and toasted in a 200° oven)
1 cup dried currants
1 cup broken pecans
¼ teaspoon ground pepper
¼ teaspoon ground cinnamon
¼ teaspoon ground sage

TURKEY:

1 fresh turkey (18 pounds)
4 tablespoons (½ stick) unsalted butter, melted
¼ cup extra-virgin olive oil
salt and pepper

BROTH AND GRAVY:

neck and giblets from the turkey (not the liver)
1 can (14 to 16 ounces) chicken broth
hot water or potato water (water in which peeled potatoes
have been boiled)
¼ cup plus 2 tablespoons all-purpose flour

1. Position the oven rack at the lowest level. Preheat the oven to 450°F.

2. Prepare the stuffing: In a large skillet, melt the butter over medium heat. Add the onion and celery and cook, stirring often, until the onion is tender, about 2 minutes.

3. Meanwhile, in a large bowl, combine the bread cubes, currants, pecans, pepper, cinnamon, and sage. Pour the onion mixture over the bread cube mixture and toss to mix. If you like a very moist stuffing, add ¼ to ½ cup warm water and toss again.

4. Prepare the turkey: Rinse the turkey inside and out under cold running water; drain well and pat dry with paper towels. Loosely fill the cavity of the turkey with the stuffing. Tie the wings and legs close to the main body of the turkey. Mix together the butter and oil, and use some of it to brush the bird on all sides. Reserve any remaining butter mixture to baste the turkey as it roasts. Place the turkey on a rack in an open roasting pan. Sprinkle with salt and pepper.

5. Place in the oven and immediately reduce the temperature to 350°. Roast until no pink juices appear when the thickest part of the thigh is pierced with a fork, 3½ to 4 hours, or until a meat thermometer inserted in the thigh, away from the bone, registers 180° to 185°. Baste every 30 minutes with the butter-oil mixture until it runs out. Baste with the pan drippings after that.

6. While the turkey roasts, prepare the giblet broth for the gravy: In a medium saucepan over high heat, combine the turkey neck and giblets with the chicken broth. Bring to a boil. Reduce the heat to a simmer, cover, and cook until the neck and giblets are tender, about 1½ hours. Remove from the heat and let stand until cool enough to handle. Cut the meat from the neck and chop it and the giblets into small pieces, discarding any gristle. Store separately from the broth. Cool and refrigerate both until ready to use.

7. When the turkey is done, remove to a warm platter. Let stand while preparing the gravy.

8. Prepare the gravy: When the turkey has been removed from the roasting pan, pour the drippings into a measuring cup, scraping up any browned bits that cling to the pan. Skim off 4 tablespoons of the fat from the top and place in a medium saucepan. Discard the remaining floating fat. Combine the defatted drippings with the giblet broth. Add enough hot water or potato water to measure 4 cups. Add the flour to the fat in the saucepan and cook over medium heat, stirring constantly, for 3 minutes. Stir in the broth mixture and cook, stirring, until thickened, about 2 minutes. Stir in the chopped meat from the turkey neck and giblets. Cook, stirring now and then, until heated through, 2 to 3 minutes.

Serving suggestion: Carve the turkey and arrange the slices on a warmed serving platter. Serve the gravy in a warmed sauceboat on the side. Spoon the stuffing directly from the cavity of the bird. (Be sure to remove all stuffing from the bird before refrigerating any leftovers.) Traditional with Mom's Mashed Potatoes.

Turkey and Gravy Express

My good friend, Ilse Fliesser, prepares her Thanksgiving turkey by this method. Technically, the turkey is steamed rather than roasted, but the meat, including the breast, is moist and flavorful.

SERVES 12

1 fresh turkey (10 to 12 pounds)
salt and pepper
1½ cups chicken broth
½ cup cold water
3 tablespoons cornstarch

1. Preheat the oven to 400°F.

2. Remove the neck and giblets from the turkey and reserve for another use. Rinse the turkey under cold running water; drain well and pat dry with paper towels. Sprinkle lightly, inside and out, with salt and pepper. Tie the wings and legs close to the main body of the bird. Place on a rack in a covered roaster. Pour the broth around, not on, the turkey.

3. Cover the roaster and bake until no pink juices appear when the thickest part of the thigh is pierced with a fork, about 2 hours, or until a meat thermometer inserted in the thigh, away from the bone, registers 180° to 185°. Tilt the bird as you lift it from the pan to allow any trapped juices to run into the broth in the pan. Place the turkey on a warmed platter and let stand while preparing the gravy.

4. Pour the broth from the roaster into a 4-cup measuring cup. Spoon off any excess fat from the broth. Add enough chicken broth or water to measure 3 cups. Pour this broth mixture into a medium saucepan and bring to a simmer over medium heat. Stir together the cold water and cornstarch until smooth; stir into the simmering broth. Cook, stirring constantly, until thickened, about 2 minutes. Add salt and pepper to taste.

Serving suggestion: Carve the turkey and arrange slices on a warmed serving platter. Serve the gravy in a warmed sauceboat on the side. Good with Mom's or Olive Oil Mashed Potatoes.

Wooden Spoon Kitchen Wisdom: Roasting Times for Turkey

It is almost impossible to accurately predict when a turkey will be ready from the oven. So many factors are involved—the age of the bird, its fat content, how cold it is when you place it in the oven, etc. I have noticed a trend toward the breeding of more tender turkeys that take less roasting time than in years past. A general guideline would be to allow 15 minutes per pound for birds weighing 12 to 16 pounds; 12 minutes per pound for those over 16 pounds. Turkeys that are stuffed can take 30 minutes longer than those that are not.

Creamed Turkey Casserole

The simplest way to reheat leftover turkey is to layer it in its own gravy, cover it, and simmer or bake until heated through. When you have turkey left but no gravy, a casserole moistened with white sauce is a tasty way to go.

SERVES 6

3 cups cubed cooked turkey
1 cup frozen peas
1 jar (2.5 ounces) sliced mushrooms, drained
1 jar (2 ounces) chopped pimiento, drained
Double recipe of White Sauce (page 141), using 2 cups milk,
    4 tablespoons butter, and 4 tablespoons flour
2 slices bread
2 teaspoons unsalted butter

1. Preheat the oven to 350°F.

2. Place the turkey, peas, mushrooms, and pimiento in a 3-quart casserole. Prepare the white sauce. Pour over the turkey and vegetables and stir gently to mix.

3. Spread the bread with the butter. Tear the bread into several pieces and process in a food processor to make crumbs. Sprinkle the crumbs over the top of the casserole.

4. Bake, uncovered, until the top is lightly browned and the sauce is bubbling and hot, 30 to 45 minutes.

Serving suggestion: Spoon directly from the casserole onto plates. Good with Fruity Waldorf or Fruit Salad with Honey-Poppy Seed Dressing.

End-of-the-Turkey Soup

This warming soup is restorative after the hectic activity of gathered families for the holidays. The broth can be used in any soup that calls for chicken broth, but this combination is an especially nice one.

SERVES 8

TURKEY BROTH:
1 turkey carcass (from an 18-pound roast turkey)
3 quarts cold water
1 onion, quartered
1 carrot, cut into chunks
1 celery rib, cut into chunks
4 peppercorns
1 bay leaf
1 sprig parsley

SOUP:
1 medium onion, finely chopped
2 carrots, diced
1 tablespoon chopped fresh parsley
1 cup frozen green beans
1 cup frozen green peas
½ recipe Homemade Egg Noodles (page 98), or 4 ounces
    store-bought egg noodles
2 to 3 cups diced cooked turkey
salt and pepper

1. Prepare the turkey broth: Break the turkey carcass into pieces; rinse away any stuffing that may have adhered. Put in a 5- to 6-quart stockpot and add the cold water, onion, carrot, celery, peppercorns, bay leaf, and parsley. Bring slowly to a boil. Reduce the heat to a simmer, partially cover the pot, and cook for 2 to 3 hours (exact timing is not critical).

2. Strain the broth; pour into quart jars. Cool, uncovered, to room temperature. Cover and refrigerate until well chilled. Remove any solidified fat before making soup.

3. Prepare the soup: In a 5- to 6-quart stockpot, combine the turkey broth with the onion, carrots, and parsley. Cover and simmer until the vegetables are tender, 15 to 20 minutes. Add the beans, peas, and noodles, and simmer just until the noodles are tender, 7 to 10 minutes. Add the diced turkey and heat through, 3 to 5 minutes. Add salt and pepper to taste.

Serving Suggestion: Serve in heavy pottery bowls. Good with Perfect Potato Bread or Sweet Buttermilk Muffins.

Roast Turkey Breast with Under-the-Skin Pesto

Turkey breasts are so low in fat that they tend to dry out unless they are basted while cooking. The pesto used here self-bastes the turkey as it bakes. If there are any leftovers, they are wonderful for sandwiches.

SERVES 4 TO 6

½ turkey breast with skin and bone (2½ pounds)
¼ cup Pesto (page 139), or ¼ cup store-bought pesto

1. Preheat the oven to 350°F.

2. Run your fingers under the skin of the turkey to loosen it from the meat, taking care not to loosen it completely on all sides. Using your fingers, smear the pesto evenly over the meat under the skin. Stretch the skin, if necessary, to cover the pesto.

3. Place the turkey breast on a rack in a roasting pan. Bake in the oven until no pink remains when the meat is cut into, about 1 hour.

Serving suggestion: Slice the turkey breast across the grain and arrange slices on a warmed serving platter. Good with Polenta or Risotto.

Simple Baked Chicken

This is one of the easiest ways to fix a whole fryer—also one of the best.

SERVES 4

1 whole fryer (3 to 3½ pounds)
salt and pepper
1 tablespoon unsalted butter, melted

1. Preheat the oven to 450°F.

2. Remove any giblets from the chicken and reserve for another use. Rinse the chicken under cold running water; drain well and pat dry with paper towels. Pour a small amount of salt into the palm of one hand and use it to rub salt into the surface of the cavity of the chicken. Sprinkle the cavity lightly with pepper. Tie the wings and legs close to the main body of the chicken. Place breast-side up on a rack in a roasting pan. Brush the melted butter over the skin of the chicken. Sprinkle lightly with salt and pepper.

3. Place the bird in the oven and immediately reduce the oven temperature to 350°. Bake until no pink juices appear when the thickest part of the thigh is pierced with a fork, 1 to 1½ hours, or until a meat thermometer inserted in the thigh, away from the bone, registers 180° to 185°.

Serving suggestion: Carve the chicken and place serving pieces on plates. Good with Butter-Baked Potatoes or New Potatoes with Fresh Dill.

Roast Chicken with Simple Bread Stuffing

This recipe is for a 5- to 7-pound roasting chicken. Be careful not to pick up a stewing hen, as it would be tough if roasted. If you have trouble finding a large bird for roasting, use a smaller one, 3½ to 4 pounds and simply allow less time for roasting.

SERVES 6 TO 8

STUFFING:

2 tablespoons unsalted butter
⅓ cup finely diced celery
⅓ cup finely diced onion
2 cups coarsely torn, soft bread crumbs

CHICKEN:

1 roasting chicken (5 to 7 pounds)
salt and pepper
1 tablespoon unsalted butter, melted

GRAVY:

1 can (14 to 16 ounces) chicken broth
2 tablespoons cornstarch
¼ cup cold water
salt and pepper

1. Preheat the oven to 450°F.

2. Prepare the stuffing: In a skillet, melt the butter over medium heat. Add the celery and onion and cook, stirring, until the onion is tender, about 2 minutes. Add the bread crumbs and stir to mix. Remove from the heat.

3. Prepare the chicken: Remove the giblets from the cavity of the chicken and reserve for another use. Rinse the chicken under cold running water; drain well and pat dry with paper towels. Pour a small amount of salt into the palm of one hand and use it to rub salt into the surface of the cavity of the chicken. Sprinkle the cavity lightly with pepper. Loosely fill the bird with the stuffing. Tie the wings and legs

close to the main body of the chicken. Place breast-side up on a rack in a roasting pan. Brush the melted butter over the skin of the chicken. Sprinkle lightly with salt and pepper.

4. Place the bird in the oven and immediately reduce the oven temperature to 350°. Bake until no pink juices appear when the thickest part of the thigh is pierced with a fork, 2 to 2¾ hours, or until a meat thermometer inserted in the thigh, away from the bone, registers 180° to 185°. Transfer to a platter and let stand while preparing the gravy.

5. Prepare the gravy: After the chicken is removed from the roasting pan, suction or spoon off most of the fat. Add the broth to the pan and stir over medium heat to loosen any browned bits on the bottom. Bring the broth to a simmer. Stir together the cornstarch and cold water; stir into the broth mixture. Cook, stirring, until thickened, 2 minutes. Remove from the heat. Taste and add salt and pepper, if needed. Strain into a warmed sauceboat.

Serving suggestion: Carve the chicken and arrange the slices on a warmed serving platter. Serve the gravy on the side. Spoon the stuffing directly from the cavity of the bird. (Be sure to remove all stuffing from the bird before refrigerating any leftovers.) Perfect with Mom's Mashed Potatoes.

Roasted Chicken and Vegetables

With this recipe you make most of your dinner in one pan, with very little preparation.

SERVES 4

1 fryer (about 3 pounds), quartered
2 medium onions, peeled and quartered
2 large potatoes, peeled and quartered
4 medium carrots, scrubbed and left whole
2 tablespoons water
2 tablespoons unsalted butter, melted
1 tablespoon chopped fresh rosemary or 1 teaspoon dried
salt and pepper

1. Preheat the oven to 350°F.

2. Rinse the chicken under cold, running water; drain well and pat dry with paper towels. Arrange the chicken quarters and the vegetables in a single, snug layer in a shallow roasting or baking pan. Pour the water into the pan. Brush the chicken and vegetables with the melted butter. Sprinkle the rosemary and salt and pepper over all.

3. Roast until the vegetables are tender and the juices run clear when the chicken is pierced with a fork, about 1¼ hours.

Serving suggestion: Serve directly from the roasting pan. Good with Tossed Green Salad or Wilted Lettuce Salad.

Country-Fried Chicken with Milk Gravy

I like to let my fried chicken finish cooking in a slow oven so that it doesn't dry out like it does when you fry it to death. By frying the thickest pieces first, thereby allowing them the longest oven time, you end up with all of the pieces evenly moist and flavorful.

SERVES 4

CHICKEN:

1 fryer (about 3 pounds), cut up
¾ cup all-purpose flour
½ teaspoon salt
¼ teaspoon pepper
¼ cup canola oil
4 tablespoons (½ stick) unsalted butter

GRAVY:

3 tablespoons all-purpose flour
1½ cups milk, heated to hot
salt and pepper

1. Preheat the oven to 275°F. Place a flat rack in a broiler pan.

2. Prepare the chicken: Rinse the chicken under cold, running water; drain well and pat dry with paper towels. Place the flour, salt, and pepper in a sack (I use plastic), and shake to mix. Heat the oil and butter over medium-high heat in a large skillet. Working with 1 piece at a time, shake the chicken in the flour-filled sack to coat with the flour mixture. Starting with the largest pieces first and taking care not to crowd the pan, brown the chicken on both sides in the oil-butter mixture. As the pieces are browned, remove them to the rack in the roasting pan and place in the oven. (Reduce the heat under the skillet if the pieces begin to brown too fast.) The larger pieces will be cooking in the oven while the smaller pieces are being browned.

3. Continue to bake until the largest pieces are cooked through, 15 to 20 minutes.

4. When all of the chicken is just about cooked through, prepare the gravy: Spoon off all but 3 tablespoons of the drippings in the skillet. Stir in the flour. Cook over medium heat, stirring, until smooth, about 1 minute. Stir in the hot milk and cook, stirring, until thickened, 2 to 3 minutes. Add salt and pepper to taste.

Serving Suggestion: Transfer the pieces of chicken to a warmed serving platter. Pour some of the gravy over the chicken and serve the rest in a warmed sauceboat. This is wonderful with Mom's Mashed Potatoes or Polenta.

Smothered Chicken

At first glance, this sounds like the fried chicken above, but a closer look lets you see that it isn't. The chicken in this recipe is fried until browned, steamed in the skillet to finish the cooking, smothered in a creamy gravy, and baked for a sumptuous finish.

SERVES 4

CHICKEN:
1 fryer (about 3 pounds), cut up
½ cup all-purpose flour
½ teaspoon salt
¼ teaspoon pepper
½ cup canola oil

GRAVY:
3 tablespoons all-purpose flour
2 cups light cream or half-and-half
salt and pepper

1. Prepare the chicken: Rinse the chicken under cold, running water; drain well and pat dry with paper towels. Mix the flour with the salt and pepper in a shallow bowl or pie plate. Dredge the chicken on all sides in the flour, shaking off any excess. Heat the oil in a large skillet over medium-high heat. A few pieces at a time, brown the chicken in the hot oil on all sides; remove the pieces as they are browned.

2. Preheat the oven to 300°F.

3. When all of the chicken pieces are browned, reduce the heat to low and return all of the chicken to the skillet. Cover and cook for 20 minutes. Transfer the chicken to a large flat casserole.

4. Prepare the gravy: Pour off the fat from the skillet. In a bowl, stir together the flour and half-and-half until smooth. Pour into the skillet, and cook over medium heat, stirring often, until smooth and thickened, about 3 minutes. Add salt and pepper to taste.

5. Pour the gravy over the chicken. Cover the casserole and bake until the chicken is heated through, 15 to 30 minutes.

Serving suggestion: Serve the chicken directly from the casserole. Good with Long-Grain or Brown Rice.

Oven-Fried Chicken

Here's yet another way to produce fried chicken. I like this method because there is little chance of grease spattering your clothes while you cook. The chicken is as crisp as that prepared on stovetop.

SERVES 4

3 pounds meaty chicken parts (breast halves, drumsticks,
*   and thighs)*
1¼ cups buttermilk
1 large egg, beaten
1½ teaspoons Tabasco sauce
1 cup all-purpose flour
¼ cup stone-ground cornmeal
1 teaspoon salt
½ teaspoon pepper
½ teaspoon paprika
1½ cups corn oil

1. Rinse the chicken under cold running water; drain well and pat dry with paper towels. Place in a single layer in a shallow dish or pan. Mix together the buttermilk, egg, and Tabasco; pour over the chicken. Let stand for 30 minutes to marinate.

2. Line a baking sheet with waxed paper. In a shallow bowl, mix the flour with the cornmeal, salt, pepper, and paprika. Working with 1 piece at a time, lift the chicken and let some of the marinade drip away. Coat the chicken with the flour mixture and place on the lined baking sheet. When all of the pieces are coated, cover the chicken lightly with additional waxed paper. Refrigerate until chilled, about 1 hour.

3. Meanwhile, preheat the oven to 450°F.

4. Place the oil in a large shallow roasting pan (about 15×10 inches). Heat in the oven until the oil is hot, about 5 minutes.

5. Remove the pan from the oven; arrange the chilled chicken, skin sides down, in the oil. Bake for 20 minutes.

6. Remove the pan from the oven, and turn the chicken with tongs. Return to the oven and bake until browned all over, 15 to 20 minutes longer.

Serving suggestion: Transfer the chicken to a warmed platter for serving. Good with an assortment of salads and side dishes, such as Refrigerator Coleslaw, Creamy Potato Salad, and Sautéed Apples.

Teriyaki Chicken with Broiled Pineapple

Teriyaki chicken is a popular restaurant entrée. It's easy to duplicate at home, complete with the pineapple garnish. Buy already peeled and cored pineapple to give you a head start.

SERVES 4

4 boneless, skinless chicken breast halves
⅓ cup bottled teriyaki sauce
3 scallions, thinly sliced, including some of the green
4 peeled and cored pineapple rings

1. Preheat the oven to 350°F.

2. Place the chicken in a nonreactive baking pan or dish. Pour the teriyaki sauce over the chicken. Turn the chicken over once to coat both sides. Sprinkle the scallions over the top. Let stand to marinate while preheating the oven, about 15 minutes.

3. Bake the chicken for 15 minutes. Remove from the oven; preheat the broiler.

4. Remove the chicken from the marinade and place on a broiler pan. Cut the pineapple into 4 slices and place around the chicken. Brush both the chicken and pineapple with additional marinade. Broil, turning once, until lightly browned on both sides, 2 to 3 minutes per side.

Serving suggestion: Place the chicken on serving plates and top with the pineapple slices. Good with Noodle-Rice Pilaf.

Chicken and Noodles

I prefer chicken thighs for this dish rather than breasts, because chicken breasts have a tendency to dry out when boiled in broth.

SERVES 4 TO 6

1 teaspoon extra-virgin olive oil
1 medium onion, finely chopped
1 medium carrot, finely chopped
2 cans (each 14 to 16 ounces) chicken broth
1½ pounds boneless skinless chicken thighs
1 tablespoon finely chopped parsley
1 recipe Homemade Egg Noodles (page 98), or 8 ounces
  store-bought noodles

1. In a heavy medium saucepan, heat the oil over medium heat. Add the onion and carrot, partially cover, and cook, stirring often, until the onion is soft and the carrot is tender, 3 to 5 minutes. Add the chicken broth, chicken, and parsley. Reduce the heat to a simmer, cover, and cook until the juices run clear when the chicken is pierced with a fork, about 20 minutes.

2. Add the noodles, cover, and simmer until the noodles are tender, 7 to 10 minutes.

Serving suggestion: Serve in shallow soup plates. Good with Pea and Peanut Salad and Summer Tomatoes Dressed with Basil.

Country Captain

Country Captain supposedly got its name from the sea captain who learned of it from an Indian officer during his voyages back and forth to America's shores. Both Irma Rombauer *(Joy of Cooking)* and James Beard *(James Beard's American Cookery)* refer to this bit of history, with credits to Cecily Brownstone for the research. I have always thought of it as a Southern recipe, but that's probably because I first ate it in the South. Nonetheless, it is a mild-flavored curry that can be served for company meals as well as family. Although Beard, Rombauer, and Brownstone all use green bell pepper in their recipes, I do not.

SERVES 4

1 fryer (3 pounds), cut into 8 serving pieces
⅓ cup all-purpose flour
1 teaspoon salt
¼ teaspoon pepper
2 tablespoons unsalted butter
2 tablespoons extra-virgin olive oil
1 medium onion, finely chopped
1 garlic clove, minced or pressed
1 teaspoon curry powder
1 can (14 to 16 ounces) tomatoes, with their juices
¼ cup raisins

1. Preheat the oven to 350°F.

2. The chicken should be cut to produce 2 pieces of breast, 2 drumsticks, 2 thighs, and 2 wings. Any remaining pieces should be reserved for another purpose. Rinse the chicken under cold running water; drain well and pat dry with paper towels. Mix the flour with the salt and pepper and use to coat the chicken pieces.

3. In a dutch oven or heavy stovetop-to-oven casserole, melt the butter with the oil over medium heat. Add the onion and garlic and cook, stirring, until the onion is tender, about 3 minutes. Remove with a slotted spoon.

4. Add the chicken to the oil/butter mixture and cook, turning once, until golden-brown. Remove the pieces as they brown. Pour off any remaining fat.

5. Return the onion and garlic to the pot. Sprinkle with the curry powder and stir to coat. Add the tomatoes with their juices and the raisins, and stir, breaking up the tomatoes with the side of a spoon. Return the chicken to the pot; spoon the sauce over the pieces.

6. Cover the dutch oven and bake until the chicken is tender, 45 to 60 minutes.

Serving suggestion: Serve directly from the dutch oven. Good with Long-Grain or Brown Rice and Peach Chutney.

Potatoes, Pastas, Grains, and Legumes

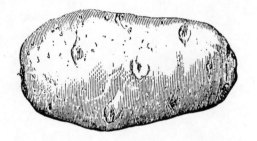

What would a meat and potatoes cookbook be without a bushelful of recipes for the potatoes themselves? From the quintessential french-fried potato to homey mashed or scalloped potatoes, every recipe you need to accompany your steaks, chops, and roasts is here. Hash Brown Potatoes with Bacon and Onions are down-home good; Butter-Baked Potatoes will make your mouth water; and New Potatoes with Fresh Dill are as fresh as the spring weather that creates them.

For variety in your meals there are recipes for homemade pasta, fluffy rice, tasty pilafs, creamy risotto, golden polenta, hearty lentils, and flavorful beans.

French-Fried Potatoes

There is nothing better than french-fried potatoes with pan-fried steaks or hamburgers. I like a touch of olive oil in the hot fat to impart just a hint of its flavor.

SERVES 4

4 medium russet potatoes
3 to 4 cups canola oil, for frying
2 tablespoons extra-virgin olive oil
salt and pepper

1. Have ready a bowl of cold water. Peel the potatoes; slice lengthwise, ¼ inch thick. Stack the slices and cut lengthwise into ¼-inch sticks. Place the sticks in the cold water.

2. Heat the oils in an electric fryer or in a deep heavy pot to 375°F. (It usually takes about 10 minutes to preheat the oil.) Thoroughly dry the potato sticks on paper towels. Drop the potatoes from a slotted

spoon into the hot oil; do not crowd the potatoes in the oil. If necessary, cook the potatoes in 2 or more batches. Fry until golden brown, about 15 minutes. Remove with a slotted spoon; drain on several thicknesses of paper towels.

3. If cooking in batches, place the first-cooked in a 200° oven to keep warm. Sprinkle with salt and pepper right before serving.

Double Fries

The crispest of fried potatoes are Double Fries. Follow the recipe for French-Fried Potatoes up to the point of frying them. Fry them, in batches if necessary, for 5 minutes only, removing them with a slotted spoon to drain and cool on paper towels. This can be done as long as 1 hour before the second frying.

When ready to fry the second time, reheat the oil to 375°F. Drop the potatoes into the hot oil and fry until crisp and golden brown, about 10 minutes. Remove with a slotted spoon and drain on several thicknesses of paper towels. Sprinkle with salt and pepper and serve immediately.

Home-Fried Potatoes

Leftover boiled potatoes can be used for this dish, but freshly boiled ones are better. Use a nonstick skillet to make it easier to keep the potatoes from sticking during cooking.

SERVES 4

4 medium russet potatoes
2 to 4 tablespoons unsalted butter
salt and pepper

1. Boil the potatoes in their skins, in water to cover, until barely tender, 15 to 20 minutes. Drain well; let stand until cool enough to handle. Peel the potatoes and slice or dice them.

2. Heat 2 tablespoons of the butter in a large nonstick skillet over medium heat. Add the potatoes and stir to coat with the butter. Fry the potatoes until browned on the bottom. Turn the potatoes over in chunks and brown the other side (time varies). Add additional butter if needed to prevent sticking, or if you prefer a richer dish. Add salt and pepper to taste. Serve hot.

Hash Brown Potatoes with Bacon and Onions

Potatoes, bacon, and onions make a mouth-watering combination.

SERVES 4

3 slices thick-sliced bacon, diced
1 small yellow onion, finely chopped
5 medium russet potatoes, peeled and cut into ¼-inch dice
salt and pepper

1. In a large skillet over medium heat, cook the bacon until browned and crisp. Add the onion and cook, stirring, until softened, about 2 minutes. Add the potatoes and stir to mix. Press into an even layer. Cover and cook over medium–low heat until the potatoes are tender, 15 to 20 minutes. You don't have to stir this but I usually do, about once every 5 minutes.

2. Uncover the pan and cook over medium heat to crisp and brown the potatoes on the bottom, 5 to 10 minutes longer. Season with salt and pepper and serve.

Butter-Baked Potatoes

I think some people are put off from eating baked potatoes because they are so large. My solution is to bake medium-size ones instead. This recipe is for those who like to eat the skin of their baked potatoes and is an adaptation of the way I ate them when I was growing up. My mother always rubbed her potatoes with vegetable shortening before baking them, but I prefer them this way, rubbed with butter.

SERVES 4

4 unblemished, medium-size, Idaho baking potatoes
4 tablespoons unsalted butter, softened
salt and pepper

1. Preheat the oven to 400°F.

2. Scrub the potatoes well; dry with paper towels. Pierce each potato in 10 to 12 places with the tip of a knife. Rub each potato with 1 tablespoon of the soft butter. Place the potatoes in a shallow baking pan large enough to hold them in one layer without crowding. Sprinkle with salt and pepper.

3. Bake in the oven for 30 minutes.

4. Turn the potatoes over and pierce once in the center. Continue baking until soft and tender, about 30 minutes longer.

5. After baking, cut the potatoes almost, but not quite, through the center. Drizzle the browned butter that has accumulated in the baking pan over the cut sides of the potatoes. Serve immediately.

Scalloped Potatoes

Scalloped potatoes have a richness that goes beyond the simple ingredients used to make them. They are a comfort food from the past that are welcome on today's table.

The secret of scalloped potatoes is to slice the potatoes uniformly thin, about ⅛ inch, layer them with sliced onion and butter, and almost cover with hot, light cream. Bake them in a moderate oven—first covered, to cook the potatoes through, and then uncovered, to slightly reduce the cream.

SERVES 6

4 cups thinly sliced, peeled russet potatoes
1 small onion, thinly sliced
salt and pepper
1 tablespoon all-purpose flour
2 tablespoons unsalted butter, slivered
1½ cups light cream or half-and-half

1. Preheat the oven to 350°F.

2. Spread half of the potatoes in a 2-quart lidded casserole dish or a shallow baking dish. Separate the onion into rings and scatter over the potatoes. Sprinkle lightly with salt and pepper. Sprinkle with the flour and dot with half of the butter. Spread the remaining potatoes over the top and dot with the remaining 1 tablespoon butter. Sprinkle again with salt and pepper.

3. Heat the cream until hot, but not bubbling. Gently pour into the casserole, near the edge, so as not to disturb the layers of potatoes and onions.

4. Cover the casserole or dish and bake for 45 minutes.

5. Uncover and bake until the top is lightly browned, about 15 minutes more. Serve immediately.

Potatoes Anna

This is a simplified version of a classic potato dish said to have been created by Adolphe Duglére and dedicated to his friend Anna Deslions. The potatoes are particularly good with roasted meats.

SERVES 4 TO 6

4 medium-to-large russet potatoes
5 tablespoons unsalted butter
salt and pepper

1. Preheat the oven to 400°F.

2. Peel the potatoes and drop into a pot of cold water. Butter a 1-quart lidded casserole or a baking dish with 1 tablespoon of the butter. Working with 1 potato at a time, pat the potato dry, slice thinly and evenly, and arrange the slices in the casserole. Dot each potato with 1 tablespoon of the butter; sprinkle with salt and pepper. Repeat with the remaining potatoes.

3. Cover and bake until the potatoes are tender and lightly browned, about 1 hour. Carefully turn out onto a warmed platter or serve directly from the casserole.

New Potatoes with Fresh Dill

When red potatoes are first available in early summer, they are a special treat. Whether you grow your own or select yours at the market, try to find small ones of similar size to use in this dish.

SERVES 4

1½ pounds small red potatoes
2 tablespoons unsalted butter
1 tablespoon chopped fresh dill
salt and pepper

1. Wash and quarter the potatoes, but do not peel. Place in a large saucepan, and add cold water to cover. Bring to a boil. Reduce the heat, cover, and simmer until the potatoes are fork-tender, about 20 minutes.

2. Drain the potatoes well. Toss with the butter and dill. Add salt and pepper to taste.

Mom's Mashed Potatoes

I grew up on mashed potatoes—real mashed potatoes. I think they're wonderful.

SERVES 6

5 large baking potatoes
about 1 cup milk or light cream
5 tablespoons unsalted butter
salt and white pepper

1. Wash and peel the potatoes; quarter the potatoes lengthwise, and cut crosswise in half. Place in a large saucepan and add cold, lightly salted water to cover. Bring to a boil over high heat. Reduce the heat, cover, and simmer until the potatoes begin to break apart, 20 to 30 minutes.

2. When the potatoes are almost done, heat the milk with the butter in a small saucepan until the milk is hot and the butter melts.

3. Drain the potatoes well. Shake the pan over low heat for a minute to dry the potatoes. Put the potatoes through a ricer or mash them with a hand-held potato masher. Gradually add the hot milk mixture to the potatoes, stirring all the while. (If you like firm mashed potatoes, use less milk; if you like them soupy, use more.) Add salt and white pepper to taste.

Olive Oil Mashed Potatoes

I first tasted olive oil mashed potatoes at Rubicon restaurant in San Francisco. They were incredibly light, and as soon as I returned home from my trip, I set about duplicating them. They're good with or without gravy.

SERVES 4

4 medium baking potatoes
about ¾ cup chicken broth
1 tablespoon extra-virgin olive oil
salt and white pepper

1. Wash and peel the potatoes; quarter the potatoes lengthwise, and cut crosswise in half. Place in a large saucepan and add cold, lightly salted water to cover. Bring to a boil over high heat. Reduce the heat, cover, and simmer until the potatoes begin to break apart, 20 to 30 minutes.

2. When the potatoes are almost done, heat the broth until hot. Drain the potatoes well. Shake the pan over low heat for a minute to dry the potatoes. Put the potatoes through a ricer or mash them with a hand-held potato masher. Stir in the olive oil. Gradually add the broth to the potatoes, stirring all the while. Add salt and white pepper to taste.

Wooden Spoon Kitchen Wisdom: Mashing Potatoes

Mashed potatoes are best beaten by hand. An electric mixer can be used, but if you process them in a food processor, you'll end up with gluey goo.

Mashed Potato Pancakes

These are an excellent reason for making "too many" mashed potatoes. They're good for breakfast, lunch, or supper.

SERVES 4

2 cups leftover, seasoned mashed potatoes
¼ teaspoon salt
pinch of pepper
pinch of nutmeg
2 large eggs, beaten
about 4 tablespoons (½ stick) unsalted butter

1. Stir the potatoes to loosen them. Add the salt, pepper, and nutmeg and stir again. Add the beaten eggs and mix until smooth.

2. In a nonstick skillet over medium-high heat, melt 1 tablespoon of the butter. Drop the potato mixture into the melted butter by heaping tablespoonfuls; do not crowd the pan. The pancakes will flatten as they cook. Cook until crisp and brown on both sides, turning once, 3 to 5 minutes total cooking time. Add additional butter as needed to cook the remaining pancakes. Serve immediately.

Roasted Sweet and White Potato Sticks

In this dish, the potatoes are coated with a flavorful combination of olive oil and butter before baking. The high oven temperature crisps the outsides of the potato sticks while the insides turn to baked-potato tenderness.

SERVES 4

2 medium white potatoes
2 medium sweet potatoes
1 tablespoon extra-virgin olive oil
1 tablespoon unsalted butter, melted
salt and pepper

1. Preheat the oven to 400°F.

2. Scrub the potatoes but do not peel; quarter them lengthwise. In a shallow baking pan or dish, large enough to accommodate all of the potatoes in one layer without crowding, stir together the oil and butter. Toss the potatoes in the oil–butter mixture to coat. Sprinkle with salt and pepper.

3. Bake until the potatoes are fork-tender and lightly browned, 30 to 45 minutes.

Creamy Potato Salad

I debated about whether to put my potato salads in this chapter or in the one devoted to salads. I decided that I think of them more as potatoes than as salads, so here they are.

SERVES 6

4 to 5 red potatoes (2 pounds), scrubbed
1 cup mayonnaise
1½ teaspoons sugar
1½ teaspoons cider vinegar
1 teaspoon prepared mustard
1 teaspoon celery seed
½ teaspoon salt
⅔ cup diced celery
¼ cup diced sweet pickles
3 scallions (white parts only), thinly sliced
2 hard-cooked eggs, coarsely chopped

1. Place the potatoes in a large saucepan and add lightly salted water to cover. Bring to a boil over high heat. Reduce the heat, cover, and simmer until tender, 25 to 30 minutes. Drain well; let stand, uncovered, until cooled to room temperature.

2. In a large bowl, stir together the mayonnaise, sugar, vinegar, mustard, celery seed, and salt. Stir in the celery, pickles, and scallions.

3. Peel and cube the cooled potatoes. Add to the mayonnaise mixture along with the chopped egg. Stir gently to mix. Cover and refrigerate until chilled. Serve cold.

Hot Potato Salad

The sweet-sour flavors of this hot potato salad echo my German heritage.

SERVES 4 TO 6

4 to 5 red potatoes (2 pounds), scrubbed
6 slices lean bacon, diced
1 medium onion, chopped
1 celery rib, diced
2 tablespoons all-purpose flour
2 tablespoons sugar
1 teaspoon salt
⅛ teaspoon pepper
⅓ cup cool water
⅓ cup cider vinegar
1 tablespoon chopped fresh parsley

1. Place the potatoes in a large saucepan and add lightly salted water to cover. Bring to a boil over high heat. Reduce the heat, cover, and cook until tender, 25 to 30 minutes. Drain well; let stand, uncovered, until cool enough to handle.

2. Meanwhile, in a large skillet over medium heat, cook the bacon until crisp. Remove with a slotted spoon and drain on paper towels. Pour off all but 2 tablespoons of the bacon drippings. Add the onion and celery and cook, stirring often, until the onion is tender, 2 to 4 minutes. Sprinkle on the flour, sugar, salt, and pepper; stir to mix. Add

the water and vinegar and cook, stirring, until thickened, 1 to 2 minutes. Remove from the heat.

3. Peel and slice the potatoes ¼ inch thick. Add to the hot dressing along with the bacon and parsley. Return the skillet to medium heat and cook, stirring gently, until heated through, 2 to 4 minutes. Serve warm.

Homemade Egg Noodles

These are the noodles that I use for End-of-the-Turkey Soup (page 71) and Chicken and Noodles (page 81). If you want to cut your cholesterol, use the extra egg white; if you want old-fashioned flavor, use the yolk.

MAKES ABOUT 8 OUNCES OR 2 MAIN-COURSE SERVINGS

1 cup unbleached all-purpose flour
1 large egg
1 large egg white, or 1 large egg yolk
1 teaspoon olive oil
¼ teaspoon salt

1. Place the flour in a large mixing bowl. For mixing, use a fork throughout.

2. In a measuring cup, beat the egg with the egg white or yolk. Add the olive oil and salt and beat until smooth. Pour the egg mixture in the center of the flour and mix with the fork until a ball of dough that cleans the bowl forms. If the dough remains dry, add water, 1 teaspoon at a time, until the dough comes together. (Sometimes you need to get your hands into the bowl to knead the flour into the dough.)

3. Knead the dough on a lightly floured surface until smooth and slightly elastic. Wrap the ball of dough in plastic wrap and let rest for 20 minutes to allow the gluten in the flour to relax.

4. On a lightly floured surface, roll out the dough to an 18×12-inch rectangle. (The dough should be slightly less than ⅛ inch

thick.) Cut with a knife or pastry wheel into ¼×12-inch strips. Transfer the strips to a wood drying rack or paper towel-lined wire racks to dry while you prepare the rest of the meal. It is not necessary to completely dry the pasta before it is cooked. (If you want to store homemade noodles or pasta, dry them until they are leathery to almost bone-dry; refrigerate in airtight plastic sacks to retard mold formation.)

Buttered Noodles

Boil homemade Egg Noodles in lightly salted water until al dente (firm to the tooth). Toss with softened unsalted butter, using as much as your conscience will allow. Add salt and pepper to taste.

Fresh Pasta

Simply follow the recipe for Homemade Egg Noodles, but call it Fresh Pasta. Boil in lightly salted water until al dente (firm to the tooth). Serve with Pesto, page 139; Fresh Tomato Sauce, page 140; or Meat Sauce, page 141.

Long-Grain Rice

The best of rice should be cooked at a simmer, so that the rice can slowly absorb the liquid it cooks in. A quick stir with a fork aerates and fluffs the cooked rice.

SERVES 4

1 cup long-grain white rice
1¾ cups cool water
½ teaspoon salt

1. Place all of the ingredients in a medium saucepan. Bring to a boil over high heat. Reduce the heat to low, cover, and simmer until all of the water is absorbed, 45 to 60 minutes. (Tilt the pan; if no water runs up to the edge of the rice, the water is absorbed.)

2. Remove from the heat and fluff with a fork.

Brown Rice

Follow the directions for Long-Grain Rice, substituting brown rice for the white and increasing the water to 2 cups.

Wild Rice

Wild rice is not really rice, but is the seed from a wild grass that grows along the edges of lakes in northern Minnesota and Wisconsin. It is still harvested by hand by Indians who bend the grasses over the sides of their canoes, beating the seeds into the bottom of the boat with paddles. Wild rice is a scarce and expensive commodity, but well worth an occasional indulgence. (There is a domesticated wild rice that is being grown commercially, but it varies from the truly wild, having a lighter color and flavor.) To mail-order wild rice, call American Spoon Foods, 800-222-5886.

SERVES 4

2½ cups water
1 cup wild rice
1 teaspoon salt

1. Pour the water into a medium saucepan and bring to a boil over high heat.

2. Meanwhile, wash the wild rice in several changes of cool water, pouring off any debris.

3. Add the rice and salt to the boiling water. Reduce the heat, cover, and simmer until the rice is tender and all or most of the water is absorbed, 40 to 45 minutes. Drain off any remaining water before serving.

Simple Rice Pilaf

Pilaf is a tasty alternative to plain rice when there is no sauce or gravy planned for the meal.

SERVES 4 TO 6

1 teaspoon extra-virgin olive oil
1 teaspoon unsalted butter
1 small onion, finely chopped
1 cup long-grain white rice
1 can (14 to 16 ounces) chicken broth
¼ cup sliced almonds
salt and pepper

1. Heat the oil and butter in a medium saucepan over medium-high heat. Add the onion and cook, stirring often, until tender, 3 to 5 minutes. Stir in the rice. Cook, stirring often, until the rice is golden, 3 to 5 minutes.

2. Protect your hands against rising steam, and stir in the chicken broth. Heat to boiling. Reduce the heat, cover, and simmer until all of the water is absorbed, about 25 minutes.

3. While the rice is cooking, toast the almonds by stirring in a dry skillet over medium-low heat until fragrant and golden, 3 to 5 minutes.

4. Right before serving, add the almonds to the rice and fluff with a fork. Add salt and pepper to taste.

Brown Rice Pilaf

Prepare as for Rice Pilaf, but substitute brown rice for the white and add ¼ cup water to the pot along with the broth.

Fruited Rice Pilaf

Prepare as for Rice Pilaf, but add 1 teaspoon curry powder to the onions with the rice. Add ½ cup raisins with the broth.

Noodle-Rice Pilaf

In this pilaf the sautéed noodles add a wonderful wheaty flavor to the basic rice and almond combination. It's one of our favorites.

SERVES 4

> 2 tablespoons unsalted butter
> 2 ounces vermicelli, broken into short lengths
> ¾ cup long-grain white rice
> 1 can (14 to 16 ounces) chicken broth
> ¼ cup slivered almonds
> salt and pepper

1. Melt the butter in a medium saucepan over medium-high heat. Add the vermicelli and cook, stirring constantly, until golden-brown, 2 to 3 minutes. Add the rice and cook, stirring, until the rice is well-coated with the butter mixture and is slightly golden, 2 to 3 minutes. Add the broth and bring to a boil. Reduce the heat, cover, and simmer until all the broth is absorbed, about 25 minutes.

2. While the rice mixture is cooking, toast the almonds by stirring them in a dry skillet over medium-low heat until golden, 3 to 5 minutes.

3. Add the almonds to the cooked rice mixture and stir with a fork to fluff. Toss with salt and pepper to taste.

Risotto

Risotto is made with a short-grained Italian rice called arborio. The hot liquid is gradually stirred into the cooking rice and results in the exquisite creamy texture for which this classic dish is known. It is especially good with veal, lamb, or chicken.

SERVES 4 TO 6

1 tablespoon unsalted butter
1 tablespoon extra-virgin olive oil
1 small onion, finely chopped
1 cup arborio rice
1 can (14 to 16 ounces) chicken broth, heated to hot
½ to 1 cup hot water
salt and white pepper
¼ cup freshly grated Parmesan cheese

1. In a medium saucepan over medium heat, melt the butter with the oil. Add the onion and cook, stirring, until tender, 2 to 3 minutes. Add the rice and cook, stirring, until the rice is golden, 3 to 5 minutes.

2. Add ½ cup of the hot broth, and cook, stirring often, until the liquid is absorbed. Continue in this manner, adding the broth ½ cup at a time, until all is used.

3. Add the water in the same way as the broth, using enough to soften the rice to your taste. Season with salt and pepper. Fold in the cheese. Serve immediately.

Polenta

Polenta is simply Italian-style cornmeal mush. It goes well with tomato-based sauces or various meat gravies.

SERVES 6

2 ⅔ cups cold water
⅔ cup stone-ground yellow cornmeal
¼ teaspoon salt
1 tablespoon unsalted butter
2 tablespoons freshly grated Parmesan cheese (optional)

1. Bring 2 cups of the water to a boil in a medium saucepan. Meanwhile, stir together the cornmeal, the remaining ⅔ cup cold water, and the salt.

2. Slowly pour the polenta mixture into the boiling water, stirring constantly. Reduce the heat to low, and cook, stirring constantly, until thickened, about 5 minutes.

3. Stir in the butter and cheese. Serve immediately.

Fried Polenta

Prepare Polenta (see above). Line a 9×5-inch loaf pan with foil; butter the foil. Transfer the hot polenta to the lined pan. Cover and chill overnight, or until firm.

Turn the polenta out of the pan; remove the foil. Cut the polenta into ½-inch-thick slices.

In a large skillet over medium heat, melt 1 tablespoon unsalted butter in 1 tablespoon olive oil. Fry the slices in the butter-oil mixture until browned and crisp, about 10 minutes per side. Add additional butter and oil as needed.

Lentils

Lentils are of the legume family, but they do not require the usual pre-soaking. When cooked they have a mild, nutty flavor. Serve them alone or paired with rice as a side dish to any type of meat.

MAKES 3 CUPS, SERVES 6

1 cup lentils
1 can (14 to 16 ounces) chicken or beef broth
¼ bay leaf
¼ teaspoon chopped fresh herbs, or a pinch of dried (choose
*   from thyme, oregano, or marjoram)*
salt and pepper

1. Rinse the lentils in cold water; drain well. Place in a medium saucepan with the broth, bay leaf, and herbs; bring to a boil over high heat. Reduce the heat, cover, and simmer until the lentils are tender, 30 to 40 minutes. Add water to the pot, if it threatens to boil dry.

2. Remove the bay leaf. Add salt and pepper to taste. Serve as is or paired with rice.

Black or Red Beans

Beans owe their popularity to their health benefits and to the wonderful flavors they add to the plate. They can be served plain, spooned over rice, or drained and mixed in with rice or vegetables.

MAKES 3 CUPS, SERVES 6

1 cup black (turtle) or red beans
3 cups cool water, for soaking
1 teaspoon extra-virgin olive oil
1 tablespoon chopped onion
1 bay leaf
3 cups cool water, for cooking
¾ teaspoon salt
dash of pepper

1. Rinse the beans in cold water; cover with 3 cups of water and soak overnight. Drain, rinse, and drain again.

2. In a large saucepan, heat the oil over medium heat. Add the onion and cook, stirring, until tender, about 2 minutes. Add the drained beans, the bay leaf, and the 3 cups water. Reduce the heat, cover, and simmer for 1 hour.

3. Add the salt and pepper. Cover and simmer until the beans are tender, 1 to 1½ hours longer.

4. Remove the bay leaf. Serve as is or paired with rice or vegetables.

Salads and Side Dishes

Salads and side dishes add balance to a meal, and their visual appeal entices the palate through the eye. The ubiquitous tossed green salad never goes out of style, but it need not be the only salad served.

Expand your green horizons with Wilted Lettuce Salad, Layered Salad, or Pea and Peanut Salad. For a slaw alternative try Chinese Cabbage with Dill Dressing, Refrigerator Coleslaw, Pineapple Slaw, or Calico Slaw. For make-ahead salads, marinate with Three-Bean Salad and Copper Pennies. Add the sweetness of fruit with Fruity Waldorf, Fruit Salad with Honey–Poppy Seed Dressing, Sautéed Apples, or Curried Fruit.

Tossed Green Salad

This simple salad, made from iceberg, leaf, romaine, or Bibb lettuce, is undoubtably the most popular anywhere in this country. Serve it as is or make additions, such as shredded carrots, quartered tomatoes, sliced mushrooms, cucumbers, or radishes.

SERVES 4

4 cups torn mixed fresh salad greens, washed and dried
¼ to ⅓ cup Basic Vinaigrette or other dressing of your choice
(pages 143–45)

Place the lettuce in a large salad bowl. Pour just enough of the dressing over the greens to moisten them. Toss gently to mix well. Serve at once.

Wilted Lettuce Salad

One of my elderly friends who no longer gardens loves Wilted Lettuce Salad. When my lettuce patch explodes with produce, I take her sacks full of crisp leaf lettuce, already washed and ready to use. She fries a little bacon, mixes it with oil and vinegar, adds just a touch of sugar, and we sit down to our early summer treat of Wilted Lettuce Salad.

SERVES 6

4 slices lean bacon
¼ cup finely chopped onion
¼ cup extra-light olive oil
¼ cup cider vinegar
1 tablespoon sugar
1 teaspoon Worcestershire sauce
6 cups washed, dried, and torn leaf lettuce leaves
salt and pepper

1. In a nonreactive large skillet over medium heat, fry the bacon until crisp. Remove to paper towels to drain.

2. Add the onion to the bacon drippings and cook until tender, 2 to 3 minutes. Stir in the olive oil, vinegar, sugar, and Worcestershire sauce. Bring to a boil, stirring constantly. Remove the pan from the heat.

3. Place the lettuce into a large salad bowl. Pour the hot dressing over the lettuce and toss gently to mix well. Sprinkle with salt and pepper to taste. Crumble the bacon over the top. Serve at once.

Layered Salad

This is written for use as a winter salad, but when the summer garden is in full swing, I substitute sliced zucchini and chopped tomatoes for the mushrooms and olives. You can toss the salad right before serving, but I prefer to display the layers, letting diners fend for themselves.

SERVES 8

boiling water
1 package (10 ounces) frozen peas
6 cups shredded or chiffonade-cut lettuce
1 cup sliced button mushrooms
1 cup pitted ripe olives
3 hard-cooked eggs, sliced
1 cup shredded sharp cheddar cheese (4 ounces)
8 slices bacon, cooked until crisp, drained, and crumbled
1½ cups mayonnaise
2 teaspoons fresh lemon juice

1. Pour enough boiling water over the peas to cover; let stand for 2 minutes. Drain well; reserve.

2. Place the lettuce in the bottom of a large glass salad bowl. Layer the peas, mushrooms, olives, eggs, cheese, and bacon over the lettuce.

3. Stir together the mayonnaise and lemon juice. Spoon the mayonnaise mixture evenly over the salad. Cover and refrigerate to chill.

Chinese Cabbage with Dill Dressing

This is a quick, creamy, slaw-like salad. The dill seeds complement the flavor of the Chinese cabbage.

SERVES 4

¼ cup mayonnaise
1 teaspoon fresh lemon juice
1 teaspoon milk
½ teaspoon dill seeds
4 cups shredded or chiffonade-cut Chinese cabbage (about 12 ounces)
salt and pepper
6 cherry tomatoes, cut in half

111

1. In a nonreactive large bowl, stir together the mayonnaise, lemon juice, milk, and dill seeds. Add the cabbage and toss to coat the cabbage with the dressing. Add salt and pepper to taste.

2. Spoon the salad onto plates. Divide the tomatoes among the plates and place to the side of the cabbage.

Refrigerator Coleslaw

I keep this on hand all summer long. It can be stored in the refrigerator for several days, so that you can dip out what you want, when you want it.

SERVES 8

1 medium head cabbage, cored and shredded
1 green bell pepper, cored, seeded, and diced
1 cup thinly sliced celery
3 scallions, thinly sliced (including some of the green tops)
½ cup white wine vinegar
1 cup sugar
1 teaspoon mustard seeds
1 teaspoon celery seeds
pepper

1. In a nonreactive large bowl, mix the cabbage with the bell pepper, celery, and scallions.

2. In another bowl, stir together the vinegar, sugar, and both types of seeds. Pour over the vegetables; mix well. Cover and refrigerate for at least 3 hours before serving.

3. Stir well each time you dish some out. Offer freshly ground pepper at serving time.

Pineapple Slaw

This is a nice light slaw that's good with barbecued ribs.

SERVES 6 TO 8

1 small head green cabbage, cored and finely shredded
1 can (15 to 16 ounces) crushed pineapple,
   packed in its own juice
1 cup mayonnaise
1 teaspoon celery seeds
¼ teaspoon salt
¼ teaspoon pepper
¼ teaspoon Tabasco sauce

1. Place the cabbage in a large bowl. Drain the pineapple well, reserving the juice. Add the pineapple to the cabbage; toss together.

2. In a small bowl, stir together the mayonnaise, celery seeds, salt, pepper, and Tabasco. Stir in 3 to 4 tablespoons of the reserved pineapple juice to make a creamy texture. Pour the dressing over the cabbage mixture and stir to mix. Cover and refrigerate until chilled. Best served within 24 hours.

Calico Slaw

Prepare Pineapple Slaw. Add ½ cup raisins and 1 carrot, finely grated. Stir to mix.

Three-Bean Salad

When you have a salad like this waiting in the refrigerator, it makes meal preparation seem a lot easier.

SERVES 10 TO 12

⅓ cup red wine vinegar
1 tablespoon sugar
1 teaspoon salt
¼ teaspoon pepper
pinch of crushed red pepper flakes
½ cup extra-light olive oil
2 cups cooked fresh green beans, or 1 can (15 ounces) cut
green beans, drained
2 cups cooked fresh wax beans, or 1 can (15 ounces) cut
wax beans, drained
1 can (15 ounces) red kidney beans, rinsed and drained
1 medium red onion, thinly sliced and separated into rings

1. In a large bowl, whisk together the vinegar, sugar, salt, pepper, and pepper flakes. Gradually whisk in the oil.

2. Add all of the beans and the onion; toss gently to mix. Cover and refrigerate until chilled. Stir again right before serving.

Pea and Peanut Salad

I first tasted Pea and Peanut Salad when vacationing in Michigan, where it is a staple on restaurant buffet tables. The combination of sweet peas, salty peanuts, and creamy dressing is positively addictive.

SERVES 4

1 package (10 ounces) frozen peas
boiling water
¼ cup mayonnaise

¼ cup sour cream
1 scallion, thinly sliced (including some of the green)
½ cup dry-roasted peanuts
salt and pepper
2 cups shredded iceberg lettuce

1. Pour the peas into a bowl and pour enough boiling water over them to cover. Let stand for 1 minute; drain well.

2. In a medium bowl, stir together the mayonnaise, sour cream, and scallion. Add the peas and stir to mix thoroughly. Cover with plastic wrap and chill until serving time.

3. Right before serving, stir the peanuts into the pea mixture. Add salt and pepper to taste. Place the lettuce on individual salad plates and spoon the pea mixture over the lettuce.

Summer Tomatoes Dressed with Basil

We can hardly wait for the first tomato to ripen, and then we have them every day until frost takes them away again.

SERVES 4 TO 6

4 large garden- or field-ripened tomatoes
¼ cup fresh lemon juice
¼ teaspoon salt
⅛ teaspoon pepper
¼ cup extra-light olive oil
6 to 8 large basil leaves, shredded or cut into chiffonade

1. Peel the tomatoes; slice onto a small platter.

2. In a small bowl, whisk together the lemon juice, salt, and pepper. Slowly whisk in the oil. Drizzle over the tomatoes; sprinkle with the basil. Serve immediately.

Wooden Spoon Kitchen Wisdom: About Tomatoes

Tomatoes will retain a better flavor if kept at room temperature. Chilling in the refrigerator robs them of that flavor. Garden and field-grown tomatoes may have a tough skin, and the tomatoes will be more attractive to serve and eat if peeled.

To peel, pour a teakettle of boiling water over the tomatoes and then rinse them quickly under cold running water. Trim the stem and blossom ends with a knife and the remainder of the skin should slip off easily.

Copper Pennies

My garden carrots all seem to mature at once, but that provides the wherewithal to keep Copper Pennies on hand for summer suppers.

SERVES 6

2 pounds carrots, peeled and sliced ¼ inch thick
1 can (8 ounces) tomato sauce
⅓ cup cider vinegar
½ teaspoon dry mustard
½ teaspoon celery seeds
¼ teaspoon salt
¼ teaspoon pepper
¼ cup extra-light olive oil
1 small onion, thinly sliced and separated into rings

1. In a medium saucepan, combine the carrots with lightly salted water to cover. Cover the pan and simmer until just crisp-tender, 5 to 7 minutes. Drain well.

2. In a nonreactive bowl, whisk together the tomato sauce, vinegar, dry mustard, celery seeds, salt, and pepper. Slowly whisk in the oil. Add the onion and carrots. Toss to coat the vegetables with the dressing. Cover and refrigerate until chilled. Toss again right before serving.

Fruity Waldorf

Traditional Waldorf salad includes walnuts, which are omitted here. I prefer the sweet flavor of fresh grapes.

SERVES 2

2 medium-size tart, crisp apples, peeled, cored, and sliced
⅓ cup diced celery
½ cup seedless red grapes, halved
2 tablespoons mayonnaise

In a medium bowl, lightly toss all of the ingredients together to coat with the mayonnaise. Serve in bowls or on iceberg lettuce leaves.

Fruit Salad with Honey–Poppy Seed Dressing

The dressing for this salad can be made ahead, but the salad ingredients should be assembled right before serving.

SERVES 6 TO 8

DRESSING:
¼ cup fresh lemon juice
¼ cup honey
½ teaspoon poppy seeds
¼ teaspoon salt
¼ teaspoon paprika
¼ teaspoon dry mustard
¼ cup extra-light olive oil

SALAD:
1 medium cantaloupe, seeded, the flesh cut into balls or diced
1 medium honeydew melon, seeded, the flesh cut into balls or diced
4 kiwi fruits, peeled and sliced
1 pint blueberries, rinsed and drained

117

1. Prepare the dressing: In a small bowl, whisk together the lemon juice, honey. poppy seeds, salt, paprika, and dry mustard. Slowly whisk in the oil. Cover and chill until ready to assemble the salad.

2. Prepare the salad: In a large bowl, combine the cantaloupe, honeydew, kiwi fruit, and blueberries. Whisk the dressing, pour over the fruit, and toss to coat. Serve immediately.

Sautéed Apples

Old-time cooks sauté apples in bacon drippings. I find the classic combination of butter and olive oil to be a delightful change.

SERVES 4

2 *large tart cooking apples*
1 *tablespoon unsalted butter*
1 *tablespoon extra-light olive oil*
2 *tablespoons firmly packed light brown sugar*

1. Peel the apples; core the whole apples without cutting them in half. Slice the apples crosswise into ¼-inch-thick rings.

2. Melt half of the butter with half of the olive oil in a large nonstick skillet over medium-high heat. Add half of the apple rings and cook, stirring and turning from time to time, until the apples are tender, 2 to 3 minutes. Remove the cooked apples to a plate. Cook the remaining apples in the remaining butter and oil.

3. When the second batch is done, return the first batch to the skillet. Sprinkle on the brown sugar; cook, stirring, until the sugar melts, 2 to 3 minutes. Serve warm.

Curried Fruit

This is a great side dish for a dinner that features roasted beef or pork.
SERVES 4 TO 6

4 cups cut-up fresh fruit (choose from peaches, pears, nectarines,
   apricots, plums, and pineapple)
½ cup firmly packed light brown sugar
1 teaspoon curry powder
4 tablespoons (½ stick) unsalted butter, melted

1. Preheat the oven to 350°F.

2. Place the fruit in a 1-quart casserole. In a small bowl, mix together the brown sugar and curry powder. Stir in the butter. Pour the sauce over the fruit.

3. Bake until the top of the fruit is lightly browned and the sauce is bubbly, about 35 minutes.

Vegetables

You will probably want to prepare most of your vegetables by simply steaming or simmering them to crisp-tenderness. They can then be dressed with lemon juice and /or butter and a sprinkling of salt, pepper, and /or freshly chopped herbs.

For the occasions when you want something beyond basic veggies, try Fresh Asparagus with Buttered Crumbs, Green Beans Amandine, Southern Green Beans, Harvard Beets, Orange-Kissed Carrots, Fresh Cauliflower with Cheddar Cheese, Country-Style Creamed Corn, Fresh Corn Pudding, Creamed Onions, or Scalloped Tomatoes. Favorite side-dish vegetables include Artichokes with Butter Sauce, Fresh Corn on the Cob, Simple Baked Onions, Baked Acorn Squash, and Fried Green Tomatoes.

Artichokes with Butter Sauce

One evening, dining with friends at one of my favorite "à la carte" restaurants in New Orleans, my eagerly anticipated artichoke arrived at the table. The woman to my right gave me a quizzical look, "What is that—and how do you eat it?" I said, "Watch."

If you've never had an artichoke, you may be puzzled, too. Here's how to eat one: Pull off one leaf at a time; dip the meaty end into the sauce; pull the leaf through your teeth, removing the soft, tender portion. Discard the remainder. The leaves become more tender as you approach the center. When all of the manageable leaves have been eaten, cut away the remaining small leaves and the fuzzy choke. Eat the remaining meaty artichoke bottom, or "heart," with a knife and fork.

SERVES 4

4 globe artichokes
4 quarts cold water
juice of 1 lemon
6 tablespoons (¾ stick) unsalted butter, melted
1 teaspoon fresh lemon juice

1. Wash the artichokes by plunging them, pointed side down, up and down in cold water. Trim the stems flush with the base of the artichoke. Peel away one or two rows of tough outer leaves near the base. No other trimming is necessary. (The sharp tips of the leaves will soften in cooking.)

2. Combine the 4 quarts cold water and the juice of 1 lemon in a nonreactive stockpot. (Artichokes turn an unattractive gray-green when cooked in iron or aluminum pots.) Immerse the artichokes, adding water if needed to cover. Let stand for 30 minutes before cooking.

3. Bring the water to a boil over high heat. Reduce the heat to maintain a strong simmer, cover, and cook until tender, 30 to 45 minutes. Test by pulling away one bottom leaf; it should come away easily and the edible portion should be tender.

4. Meanwhile, in a small bowl, stir together the melted butter and the 1 teaspoon fresh lemon juice.

5. Drain the cooked artichokes upside down. Invert and serve on individual plates with a small container of the butter sauce for each diner.

Fresh Asparagus with Buttered Crumbs

Bright, green, fresh asparagus is as wonderful raw as it is cooked. One noon, after a vigorous morning of tennis with a friend in Scottsdale, Arizona, we went back to his apartment to freshen up. My companion had some especially nice asparagus he had purchased to prepare with buttered crumbs for lunch. Ravenous from our exercise, we couldn't resist sampling just one stalk *au naturel*. That was so delightful, we found ourselves reaching for another, and another, until the bunch was gone. We went out for lunch, with plans to cook the next time.

SERVES 4

1¼ pounds fresh asparagus
boiling water
2 tablespoons unsalted butter
1 cup soft fresh bread crumbs
salt

1. Wash the asparagus by plunging up and down in cold water. Snap the ends of the stalks to remove any woody parts. Lay the asparagus in a skillet or oblong pan with all of the heads going the same way. Pour in boiling water to cover, cover the pan, and simmer just until crisp-tender, 4 to 7 minutes. Do not overcook.

2. While the asparagus is cooking, melt the butter in a skillet over medium heat. Add the bread crumbs and cook, stirring often, until the crumbs are golden brown, 2 to 3 minutes.

3. When the asparagus is done, drain well and arrange on plates. Salt lightly. Spoon the buttered crumbs over the centers of the stalks. Serve immediately.

Green Beans Amandine

This is a slightly indulgent way to fix green beans, but it's fun to splurge on calories now and then.

SERVES 6

1 pound fresh green beans, topped and tailed
2 tablespoons unsalted butter
3 tablespoons slivered almonds
salt and pepper

1. Slice the beans, end-to-end, French-style. In a medium saucepan, bring 2 to 3 cups of lightly salted water to a boil. Add the beans and cook until just crisp-tender, 5 to 10 minutes.

2. While the beans are cooking, melt the butter in a small skillet over medium heat. Add the almonds and cook, stirring often, until golden, 3 to 5 minutes.

3. When the beans are ready, drain well. Transfer to a serving platter; sprinkle with salt and pepper. Pour the buttered almonds over the seasoned beans. Serve hot.

Southern Green Beans

We used to call these "tired" beans or "shelly" beans, because the beans we used were mature enough to yield some shelled beans as well as filled pods that had to be cooked for a long time to be palatable. I have developed a preference for much younger beans and now use bacon simply as a flavoring agent for quickly cooked tender pods.

SERVES 6

1 pound fresh green beans, topped, tailed, and cut into
  1-inch pieces
4 slices lean bacon
1 small onion, finely chopped
salt and pepper

1. In a 2-quart saucepan, bring a quantity of lightly salted water to a simmer. Add the beans and simmer until crisp-tender, 7 to 10 minutes. Drain well.

2. Meanwhile, in a large skillet cook the bacon over medium heat until crisp. Remove and drain on paper towels.

3. Pour off all but 1 tablespoon of the bacon drippings. Increase the heat to medium-high, add the onion, and cook, stirring often, until tender, about 2 minutes. Crumble the bacon and add to the onions along with the beans. Cook until heated through, stirring now and then, about 2 minutes. Add salt and pepper to taste.

Harvard Beets

For everyday meals, I simply dress boiled beets with a light coating of butter and a dash of salt. But when company comes, I like to serve these ruby-red Harvard Beets.

SERVES 4 TO 6

4 medium beets with tops attached
¼ cup sugar
2 teaspoons cornstarch
¼ teaspoon salt
¼ cup cider vinegar
1 tablespoon unsalted butter

1. Rinse the beets under cold, running water and trim, leaving 2 inches of tops and the roots attached.

2. Bring a quantity of lightly salted water to a simmer in a large saucepan. Add the beets, cover, and cook the beets until fork-tender, about 45 minutes. Drain well; rinse the beets under cool, running water until cool enough to handle; slip off the skins and trim the tops and tails; dice the beets.

3. In a nonreactive saucepan, stir together the sugar, cornstarch, salt, and vinegar. Cook over medium heat, stirring, until the mixture thickens, 2 to 4 minutes. Stir in the butter until melted.

4. Add the diced beets and cook over medium-low heat, stirring now and then, until the beets are coated with the sauce and heated through, 1 to 2 minutes. Remove from heat and serve.

Orange-Kissed Carrots

Even children who don't like cooked carrots love these. It's wonderful what a little sugar will do.

SERVES 4 TO 6

1 pound carrots, cut with a rolling cut (see page 17),
  or 1 pound peeled baby carrots
¼ cup sugar
1½ teaspoons cornstarch
¼ teaspoon salt
¼ teaspoon ground ginger
¼ cup fresh orange juice
1 tablespoon fresh lemon juice
2 tablespoons unsalted butter

1. Bring a quantity of lightly salted water to a simmer in a medium saucepan. Add the carrots, cover, and cook until crisp-tender, 12 to 15 minutes. Drain well.

2. In a nonreactive saucepan, stir together the sugar, cornstarch, salt, and ginger. Stir in the orange juice and lemon juice. Cook over medium heat, stirring constantly, until the mixture thickens, 2 to 4 minutes. Stir in the butter until melted.

3. Add the carrots to the sauce and cook over medium-low heat, stirring now and then, until the carrots are coated with the sauce and heated through, 1 to 2 minutes. Remove from heat and serve.

Fresh Cauliflower with Cheddar Cheese

This is the way my husband's mother always presented her cauliflower. It's as beautiful as it is delicious.

SERVES 6 TO 8

1 whole head fresh cauliflower
⅓ cup finely grated sharp cheddar cheese

1. Trim all the leaves and the stem from the cauliflower; trim any discolored spots.

2. In a 5- to 6-quart stockpot, bring enough lightly salted water to cover the cauliflower to a boil over high heat. Reduce the heat to a simmer, submerge the cauliflower, and cook until just fork-tender, about 10 minutes.

3. Drain the cauliflower well. Lift carefully with 2 large spoons and transfer to a serving bowl. Sprinkle the cheese over the top of the cauliflower. (The heat from the cauliflower will melt the cheese.) Serve immediately, cutting the head into wedges for each diner.

Fresh Corn on the Cob

We always say that if you want really good corn on the cob, you should start the pot of water boiling before you go out in the field to pick the corn. Actually, fresh corn that has been cleaned and well wrapped in plastic can be kept in a crisper for one or two days before cooking.

SERVES 4

4 to 8 ears fresh sweet corn
unsalted butter
salt and pepper

1. Bring a large pot of water to a boil. Drop the ears into the boiling water. Cover and cook for 2 to 5 minutes, depending on the maturity of the corn.

2. Remove the ears with tongs to serve. Pass the butter, salt, and pepper at the table.

Sautéed Corn

When we boil corn on the cob, there's always some left over. The next day we cut the kernels from the cobs to make Sautéed Corn.

SERVES 4

> *2 tablespoons unsalted butter*
> *5 ears leftover Fresh Corn on the Cob (above), kernels cut off*
> *salt and pepper*

1. In a nonstick skillet over medium-high heat, melt the butter. Add the corn kernels and cook, stirring often, until the corn is heated through and just beginning to brown. Don't let it get too browned, or it may begin to taste burned.

2. Serve the corn hot, and pass salt and pepper at the table.

Country-Style Creamed Corn

This recipe is for really fresh corn from the garden or farm stand. No milk or cream is used in the preparation; the scrapings from the cobs provide the creaminess needed. Corn that is not fresh-picked will not produce the desired creamy texture.

SERVES 4

> *4 ears fresh sweet corn, kernels cut off and cobs scraped (2 cups)*
> *2 tablespoons unsalted butter*
> *about ¼ cup water*
> *salt and pepper*

1. Place the corn, butter, and water in a small saucepan. Cook over medium heat, stirring often, until the corn is tender (time varies with the maturity of the corn). Add water as needed to keep the corn moist and creamy.

2. Add salt and pepper to taste and serve immediately.

Fresh Corn Pudding

It's fortunate that corn and tomatoes ripen at about the same time, because this pudding is wonderful with a salad of sliced tomatoes.

SERVES 4 TO 6

3 large eggs, beaten
5 ears fresh sweet corn, kernels cut off and cobs scraped (2½
cups)
¾ cup light cream or half-and-half
1 tablespoon sugar
1 tablespoon all-purpose flour
½ teaspoon salt
pinch of ground nutmeg
1 tablespoon unsalted butter

1. Preheat the oven to 375°F.

2. In a large mixing bowl, stir together the eggs, corn, cream, sugar, flour, salt, and nutmeg.

3. Place the butter in an 8-inch square pan or glass baking dish; place the pan in the oven until the butter melts.

4. Remove the pan from the oven; swirl to coat the bottom with the butter. Pour in the pudding batter. Return the pan to the oven and bake until a wooden toothpick inserted in the center comes out clean, 25 to 30 minutes. Serve hot.

Creamed Onions

Gentle simmering brings out the natural sweet flavor of these little pearl onions, and coating them with a nutmeg-flavored cream sauce turns them into a very special dish.

SERVES 4 TO 6

1 pound pearl onions, peeled and left whole
3 tablespoons unsalted butter
3 tablespoons all-purpose flour
1½ cups light cream or half-and-half, heated until hot
   (do not allow to boil)
¼ teaspoon salt
dash of white pepper
dash of ground nutmeg

1. Bring a quantity of lightly salted water to a simmer in a medium saucepan. Add the onions, cover, and simmer until tender, 8 to 10 minutes. Drain well.

2. Rinse and dry the saucepan. Melt the butter in it over medium heat; stir in the flour and cook, stirring, for 1 minute. Add the hot cream all at once and cook, stirring, until thickened, about 2 minutes.

3. Stir in the salt, pepper, and nutmeg. Add the drained onions and cook, stirring gently, until heated through, 1 to 2 minutes.

Simple Baked Onions

Baking onions brings out their sweet flavor. These are wonderfully simple, and simply wonderful.

SERVES 4

4 medium onions
⅓ cup water
2 tablespoons unsalted butter, melted
salt and pepper

1. Preheat the oven to 400°F.

2. Peel the onions; trim the bases flat so they will stand upright. Place the onions in a casserole large enough to accommodate them in one layer without crowding. Pour the water around the onions.

3. Cover the dish and bake until the onions are tender, about 1 hour. Using a slotted spoon carefully transfer the onions to small individual serving dishes. Pour the melted butter over the tops of the onions. Sprinkle with salt and pepper. Serve hot.

Squish-Squash Casserole

We once had a dinner party during a midsummer squash explosion. In defense of my garden I decided to come up with a dish that used some of my burgeoning produce. I served the yet-to-be-named dish to doubtful diners. They had seconds, asked for the recipe, and named it Squish-Squash Casserole.

SERVES 4 TO 6

2 cups cubed unpeeled zucchini
2 cups cubed unpeeled yellow crookneck squash
1 recipe White Sauce (page 141)
½ cup finely grated sharp cheddar cheese
1 cup soft fresh bread crumbs
2 tablespoons freshly grated Parmesan cheese
2 tablespoon unsalted butter, melted

1. Preheat the oven to 350°F.

2. Bring a quantity of lightly salted water to a simmer in a large saucepan. Add the squash and cook just until tender, about 3 minutes. Drain well; place in a 2-quart casserole or baking dish.

3. Prepare the white sauce. Stir in the cheddar cheese; pour over the squash. Sprinkle the bread crumbs over the top of the sauce. Scatter the Parmesan cheese on top of the crumbs. Pour the butter over all.

4. Bake the casserole until it is bubbling hot and the top is browned, 30 to 45 minutes. Serve hot.

Baked Acorn Squash

Acorn squash, one of the many winter squashes available from late summer to early spring, is a nice shape and size for cutting into two servings.

SERVES 4

2 acorn squashes
4 tablespoons (½ stick) unsalted butter, melted
¼ cup firmly packed light brown sugar
¼ teaspoon ground ginger
⅛ teaspoon ground nutmeg
salt and pepper

1. Preheat the oven to 375°F.

2. Cut the squashes lengthwise in half; scrape out the seeds. Brush the interior and cut sides of the squash with the melted butter. Mix the brown sugar with the ginger and nutmeg and sprinkle this mixture over the butter. Sprinkle lightly with salt and pepper. Place the squashes, cut sides up, in a shallow baking dish. Fill the dish with water to a depth of 1 inch.

3. Bake until the squashes are tender, 30 to 45 minutes.

Scalloped Tomatoes

This wonderful old-fashioned dish goes especially well with fried chicken.

SERVES 6 TO 8

3 tablespoons unsalted butter
1 tablespoon extra-virgin olive oil
1 medium onion, chopped
2 cups soft bread crumbs
6 medium field- or garden-grown tomatoes, peeled and sliced
1 teaspoon sugar
½ teaspoon salt
⅛ teaspoon pepper
1 tablespoon chopped fresh basil leaves

1. Preheat the oven to 350°F.

2. In a medium saucepan over medium-high heat, melt the butter in the oil. Add the onion and cook, stirring often, until tender, 2 to 4 minutes. Remove from the heat; stir in the crumbs.

3. In a 2-quart casserole dish, layer half of the tomatoes; sprinkle with ½ of the sugar, salt, pepper, and basil. Top with one-third of the crumb and onion mixture. Repeat the layering, using the remaining two-thirds crumbs on top.

4. Bake, uncovered, until the casserole is bubbling hot and browned on top, about 45 minutes. Serve warm.

Fried Green Tomatoes

Fried green tomatoes were largely ignored until Fannie Flagg's marvelous novel *Fried Green Tomatoes at the Whistle Stop Cafe,* was made into a movie. Then, everyone wanted to get into the act. Many recipes for this dish get rather complicated, advocating double-dipping the slices, first in a wet mixture and then in a dry. I prefer the simplicity of just coating the slices with a mixture of flour and cornmeal and frying them until they reach a golden-brown, lemony-tart goodness. Don't let them sit around after cooking, however, because they get soggy rather quickly.

SERVES 4

4 large green tomatoes
¼ cup stone-ground white or yellow cornmeal
¼ cup all-purpose flour
about 2 tablespoons unsalted butter
about 2 tablespoons extra-light olive oil
salt and pepper

1. Cut the tomatoes into ¼-inch slices. Mix the cornmeal and flour together on a flat plate.

2. In a nonstick skillet over medium heat melt 1 tablespoon of the butter in 1 tablespoon of the oil. Turn the tomato slices in the cornmeal-flour mixture to coat, knocking off any excess. Fry in batches in the butter-oil mixture until golden-brown on both sides, turning once, about 2 minutes per side.

3. Lift the fried tomatoes with a fork, letting some of the excess fat drip off before transferring them to a plate to serve. Sprinkle liberally with salt and pepper. Add additional butter and oil to the skillet as needed to fry the remaining slices. (If the cornmeal that is left behind in the skillet gets dark, wipe it out and start again.)

Sauces, Dressings, and the Like

I decided not to fill this chapter with some of the more complicated classics, such as hollandaise or béarnaise, preferring instead to give you directions for simpler things that you will want to use again and again.

Pesto is probably my favorite sauce of all—for tossing with pasta, spreading on meats, and adding zip to salad dressings and sandwich spreads. A few basil plants are all you need to make jar after jar of this delicacy all summer long. Store it in the freezer as you go, and you'll be rewarded during the off-season.

Fresh Tomato Sauce and its variation with meat is another universal sauce. Besides its obvious use on pasta, it's great for moistening leftover meats and vegetables for "recycled" meals. White sauce is a versatile sauce that forms the foundation for casseroles, soufflés, and stovetop creamed dishes. Emergency Gravy is self-explanatory. The vinaigrettes and Tomato-Bacon Dressing will freshen your salads. The chutneys and relish add depth to any meal.

Pesto

I don't use any nuts in my pesto. I like it better with just four basic ingredients—basil, garlic, Parmesan, and good-quality olive oil.

MAKES 1½ CUPS

2 large garlic cloves
4 cups loosely packed fresh basil leaves
¾ cup (3 to 4 ounces) freshly grated Parmesan cheese
about ½ cup extra-virgin olive oil

1. Drop the garlic cloves through the feed tube of a food processor while the machine is running. Stop the machine when the garlic is finely chopped. Add the basil and process until finely chopped. Add the

cheese and oil and process until a textured paste forms. Add additional oil, if needed, to make the paste spreadable.

2. Transfer the pesto to a glass jar. Run a table knife down the edges of the jar to release any air bubbles that may be trapped. Smooth the top of the pesto and pour in about 1 tablespoon oil to create a film on top (to prevent oxidation or darkening of the pesto). Cover tightly and refrigerate or freeze until ready to use.

3. After you use some of the pesto, smooth the top and replenish the oil film before returning to the refrigerator or freezer for storage.

Fresh Tomato Sauce

When my youngest son comes home during tomato season, gives me an impish grin, and says, "Mom, what say we make some fresh tomato sauce?" I know three things: He has been up hours ahead of me and already has the tomatoes picked; the bowl covered with cloth on my kitchen counter is yeast starter for a batch of bread; and before the day is out, we'll have a rack hung with strands of fresh pasta to go with the sauce.

MAKES 1 QUART

1 teaspoon extra-virgin olive oil
2 garlic cloves, minced or pressed
1 large onion, finely chopped
1 large carrot, finely chopped
4 pounds ripe tomatoes, peeled, seeded, and chopped
¼ cup dry red wine
1 tablespoon red wine vinegar
¼ cup minced parsley
½ cup chopped fresh basil leaves
½ teaspoon crushed red pepper flakes
salt and pepper

1. In a nonreactive large saucepan, heat the oil over medium heat. Add the garlic, onion, and carrot; partially cover and cook, stirring

now and then, until the onion wilts and the carrot is tender, 5 to 7 minutes.

2. Add the tomatoes, wine, vinegar, parsley, basil, and pepper flakes, and simmer, uncovered, until the sauce thickens to suit your taste (time varies with the juiciness of the tomatoes).

3. Add salt and pepper to taste. May be kept refrigerated for up to 5 days, or frozen for later use.

Meat Sauce

Follow the recipe for Fresh Tomato Sauce. In a separate pan, brown 1 pound of ground beef or ground turkey. Add the browned meat to the sauce. You can also use Italian sausages. Brown the sausages whole, slice them, and then brown the slices. Transfer them to the sauce with a slotted spoon, leaving any fat behind.

White Sauce

This is a recipe that scares many cooks, because they think it's too tricky or too time-consuming for their repertoire. It's actually a rather easy sauce to execute and one that can be used over and over again in everyday cooking.

MAKES 1 CUP

2 tablespoons unsalted butter
2 tablespoons all-purpose flour
1 cup milk, heated until hot
¼ teaspoon salt
⅛ teaspoon white pepper
dash of nutmeg (optional)

1. In a small saucepan over medium heat, melt the butter. Add the flour and cook, stirring, for 1 to 2 minutes. (This removes the raw taste of the flour.)

2. Remove the pan from heat and quickly add the hot milk, stirring all the while. Return the pan to heat and cook, stirring, until thickened, about 2 minutes. Stir in the salt, pepper, and nutmeg. Use in recipes as specified.

Emergency Gravy

This recipe comes in handy when you have leftover meat you want to sauce for a new meal, and either you didn't make gravy in the first place, or you have run out. It's a great improvement over what you can buy in a jar.

MAKES 2 CUPS

3 tablespoons unsalted butter
1 tablespoon minced onion
3 tablespoons all-purpose flour
1 can (14 to 16 ounces) beef or chicken broth, heated until hot
½ teaspoon chopped fresh herbs or a pinch of dried (thyme or
*   rosemary for beef, tarragon or marjoram for chicken)*
salt and pepper

1. In a small saucepan over medium heat, melt the butter. Add the onion and cook, stirring, until tender, about 2 minutes.

2. Sprinkle the flour over the onions. Continue to cook, stirring, for 1 minute. Stir in the broth and cook, stirring constantly, until the mixture thickens, about 2 minutes. Stir in the herbs and salt and pepper to taste. Serve hot.

Basic Vinaigrette

To make a decent vinaigrette you need about 3 times as much oil as vinegar. Rather than cutting that oil in an attempt to limit fats, I suggest making a good-tasting dressing and then using a light hand in applying it to your salad.

MAKES 1 CUP

¼ cup white or red wine vinegar
½ teaspoon salt
½ to 1 teaspoon Dijon mustard (optional)
⅛ teaspoon pepper
⅛ teaspoon paprika (optional)
¾ cup extra-light olive oil

1. In a small bowl, whisk together the vinegar, salt, mustard, pepper, and paprika. Slowly add the oil, whisking all the while.

2. Use immediately or transfer to a screw-top jar and refrigerate. Shake vigorously or whisk again before using.

Wooden Spoon Kitchen Wisdom: About Ground Pepper

If you want the incisive bite of freshly ground pepper, you will have to grind your own, adjusting your pepper mill for the grind that suits your palate. If your tastebuds are offended by the attack of freshly ground pepper, you may prefer the stuff that comes already ground in little jars from the spice section of the supermarket. This allows a mellow approach to pepper without the bothersome bite. To each his own—you choose—either one is correct.

Herbal Vinaigrette

Prepare Basic Vinaigrette (page 143). Add 1 to 4 tablespoons chopped fresh herbs at the last. (Choose from parsley, chives, tarragon, oregano, basil, or rosemary.)

Lemon Vinaigrette

Prepare Basic Vinaigrette (page 143), substituting 3 tablespoons fresh lemon juice for the ¼ cup wine vinegar.

Raspberry Vinaigrette

Prepare Basic Vinaigrette (page 143), substituting Raspberry Vinegar (below) for the wine vinegar.

Raspberry Vinegar

The first time my raspberry patch produces enough berries to have extra beyond daily meals, I make Raspberry Vinegar. I use it to make Raspberry Vinaigrette for Tossed Green Salad. A few fresh raspberries look pretty on top of the salad.

MAKES 1½ CUPS

½ pint (1 cup) fresh red raspberries
1½ cups white wine vinegar

1. Scald a well-washed quart jar by over-filling with boiling water; drain well. Wash the berries gently; drain well. Place the drained berries in the jar.

2. In a nonreactive saucepan, heat the vinegar until hot but not boiling. Pour over the berries. Cover loosely and let stand for 12 hours.

3. Strain the vinegar through a sieve lined with dampened cheesecloth. Pour into a 12-ounce clear bottle, cap, and store in a cool, dark place.

Tomato–Bacon Dressing

This is a zesty dressing that is agreeably low in fat.

MAKES 1⅔ CUPS

1 can (8 ounces) tomato sauce
¼ cup cider vinegar
dash of Tabasco sauce
2 tablespoons firmly packed light brown sugar
2 teaspoons dry mustard
¼ teaspoon salt
¼ teaspoon pepper
½ cup extra-light olive oil
4 slices crisply cooked bacon, crumbled

1. In a small bowl, whisk together the tomato sauce, vinegar, Tabasco, brown sugar, dry mustard, salt, and pepper. Slowly add the oil, whisking all the while. Cover and refrigerate until ready to serve.

2. Right before serving, stir in the bacon. (I sometimes reserve the bacon to sprinkle on top of the salad after it is dressed.)

Peach Chutney

This is good with roast lamb, pork, or poultry, and is absolutely essential with any kind of curry.

MAKES 4 PINTS

8 cups peeled chopped peaches (about 4 pounds)
1 cup dark raisins
1 cup golden raisins
1 cup finely chopped onions
1 cup cider vinegar
1½ cups firmly packed light brown sugar
2 garlic cloves, minced or pressed
1 tablespoon minced fresh ginger
1 teaspoon ground ginger
1 teaspoon mustard seeds
1 teaspoon salt
1 teaspoon ground cinnamon
½ teaspoon ground cloves
½ teaspoon crushed red pepper flakes

1. Combine all of the ingredients in a 5- to 6-quart nonreactive stockpot or kettle. Bring to a boil over high heat, stirring all the while. Reduce the heat and simmer, stirring often, until the peaches are translucent and the mixture thickens, 20 to 30 minutes.

2. Ladle the chutney into 4 sterilized pint jars and seal. Process the jars in a boiling water bath for 10 minutes; store the cooled jars in a dark, cool place. Alternately, store unprocessed jars in the refrigerator for up to 6 weeks.

Tomato-Apple Chutney

Make this in late summer when tomatoes are plentiful and fall apples are still green. I particularly like to serve it with pork or ham.

MAKES 2 PINTS

6 medium-size firm ripe tomatoes, peeled, seeded, and
    chopped
6 medium-size tart green apples, peeled, cored, and sliced
1 medium onion, chopped
1 cup raisins
¾ cup cider vinegar
¾ cup granulated sugar
¾ cup firmly packed light brown sugar
1 teaspoon ground ginger
½ teaspoon mustard seeds
¼ teaspoon crushed red pepper flakes

1. Combine all of the ingredients in a 5- to 6-quart nonreactive stockpot or kettle. Bring to a boil over high heat, stirring all the while. Reduce the heat to a simmer and cook, stirring often, until the apples are tender and the mixture thickens, 20 to 30 minutes.

2. Ladle the chutney into 2 sterilized pint jars and seal. Process the jars in a boiling water bath for 10 minutes; store cooled jars in a dark, cool place. Alternately, store unprocessed jars in the refrigerator for up to 6 weeks.

Sweet Cucumber Relish

This is easy to make any time you have a few extra cucumbers. It has a nice light flavor that's perfect for supper on the deck.

MAKES 5 HALF-PINTS

4 cups chopped cucumbers
2 cups chopped onions
1 green bell pepper, cored, seeded, and chopped
3 tablespoons pickling salt
cold water
2 cups sugar
1½ cups distilled white vinegar
1 teaspoon celery seeds
1 teaspoon mustard seeds

1. In a large glass or enamel bowl, mix together the cucumbers, onions, bell pepper, and pickling salt. Let stand for 2 hours.

2. Add enough cold water to cover the vegetables and stir to mix; drain well.

3. In a nonreactive 3- to 5-quart stockpot or kettle, stir together the sugar, vinegar, celery seeds, and mustard seeds; bring to a boil over high heat. Add the drained vegetables and bring back to a boil. Reduce the heat to a simmer and cook, stirring now and then, until the mixture thickens, 20 to 30 minutes.

4. Pour into 5 hot, sterilized half-pint jars and seal. Process the jars in a boiling water bath for 10 minutes; store cooled jars in a dark, cool place. Alternately, store unprocessed jars in the refrigerator for up to 6 weeks.

Breads, Rolls, and Biscuits

You would think that, after as many bread recipes as I have penned over the years, I might be "out of" recipes for bread. Actually there's nothing easier for me to do than come up with yet another idea for making what remains my favorite food—bread.

A Peasant Loaf is my response to the many times I have been asked how to make a nutty grain-flavored loaf of bread with a chewy crust—the kind of bread you can use to sop up juices on your plate or enjoy solo with a glass of red wine. Perfect Potato Bread calls for a boiled grated potato, which is easier and more reliable than mashed potatoes, and Orange-Fennel Rye Bread is just sweet enough to be enticing. For homemade rolls, you won't find anything easier than Porch Supper Pan Rolls, and for real creature comfort, try Old-Fashioned Dinner Rolls. For quick breads there's Pick-Your-Color Corn Bread, Square Soda Biscuits, and Sweet Buttermilk Muffins.

A Peasant Loaf

I am often asked how to make a really good loaf of bread. If you mean bread with a nutty, grain-flavored interior and a chewy crust, this is the recipe for you. It starts with a batter-like starter that uses only enough yeast to allow the dough to rise slowly, giving it time to develop a grainy flavor. Since there is little fat or sugar used in the dough, the water gains more importance. If yours has the taste of chlorine or other chemicals, you may want to use bottled spring water instead.

If you want to find naturally good, fresh flour, processed without chemicals, try mail-order. I keep going back to Great Valley Mills, 800-688-6455 and Walnut Acres, 800-433-3998. If you want to keep Peasant Flour on hand, mix it up by the pound rather than by the cup, using 2 parts unbleached all-purpose flour to 1 part each of bread flour and stone-ground whole wheat flour.

I list the optimum temperatures for the major ingredients in this recipe. The spiral-shaped 8-inch diameter basket I use for the last rising is called a banneton, but any closely woven round basket of like size can be used as long as it is lined with cloth that is well-rubbed with flour.

Preheated baking stones or quarry tiles help to produce a proper bottom crust. A baker's peel (shaped like an oversized ping-pong paddle) assists the transfer of the loaf from the basket to the baking stone. A rimless cookie sheet can be substituted for the baker's peel, although it is a bit more awkward to handle. If you lack both the baking stone and baker's peel, you can bake the bread on a baking sheet, transferring it directly from the basket to the sheet. The bottom crust of the loaf will not be quite as thick and chewy.

Some bakers spray the interior of the oven repeatedly with water to further crisp the crust. I find this counterproductive because heat escapes every time the oven door is opened. This is a lengthy introduction to a recipe, but I think it answers the questions I am most often asked about this type of bread.

MAKES 1 LOAF

PEASANT FLOUR:
1½ cups (or pounds) unbleached all-purpose flour
¾ cup (or pound) bread flour
¾ cup (or pound) stone-ground whole wheat flour

BREAD:
1¼ cups lukewarm (85° to 90°) water
1 envelope (2¼ teaspoons) active dry yeast (not fast-acting),
*   at room temperature (68° to 75°)*
1 teaspoon granulated sugar
3 cups Peasant Flour (see above), at room temperature
*   (68° to 75°)*
1 teaspoon salt
1 teaspoon canola oil
unbleached flour, for kneading
1 teaspoon shortening, for greasing the bowl

1. Prepare the Peasant Flour: Mix the flours together in a large container. Tightly cover and store in a cool place.

2. Prepare the bread: In a large mixing bowl (stoneware preferred), stir together the warm water, yeast, sugar, and 1½ cups of the Peasant Flour. Beat well with a wooden spoon. (Use a wooden spoon throughout.) Cover with plastic wrap and let stand at room temperature for 4 to 8 hours.

3. Stir in the salt and oil. Gradually add the remaining 1½ cups flour to make a stiff, but still somewhat sticky dough. Turn out on a well-floured surface and knead gently until the dough is smooth and elastic, letting the dough pick up only enough flour to prevent sticking, 5 to 10 minutes.

4. Rinse and dry the bowl; grease it with the shortening. Place the dough into the bowl and turn once to grease the top. Cover with plastic wrap and let rise at room temperature until doubled in bulk, 1 to 1½ hours.

5. Punch down the dough. Pull down the sides of the dough and tuck under to shape into a ball and place, top-side down, in a banneton or basket lined with a flour-impregnated cloth. Dust the loaf lightly with flour, cover with plastic and cover the plastic with a clean cloth. Let rise until doubled in bulk, about 1 hour.

6. Meanwhile, place a baking stone or quarry tile on the center shelf of the oven, leaving a margin around the edges for circulation of air. Preheat the oven to 450°F.

7. When the loaf has risen, uncover the basket and place a floured baker's peel lightly on top of the loaf; quickly invert the loaf onto the peel. Sift a light dusting of flour over the top of the loaf. Slash the loaf twice, cutting ¼-inch deep with a very sharp knife or single-handled razor blade. With a quick jerking action, slip the loaf from the peel to the baking stone.

8. Close the oven door, reduce the oven heat to 375°, and bake until the loaf is browned on top and sounds hollow when tapped on the bottom, 35 to 40 minutes. Cool on a wire rack.

Perfect Potato Bread

Many recipes for potato bread start with mashed potatoes, but this calls for a boiled grated potato—more convenient if you don't serve mashed potatoes that often. The bread is delicious.

MAKES 3 LOAVES

1 medium russet potato, peeled and grated
3 cups cold water
¼ cup plus 1 teaspoon solid vegetable shortening
¼ cup sugar
1 tablespoon salt
1 envelope (2¼ teaspoons) active dry yeast (not fast-acting)
½ cup warm (100° to 105°) water
8 to 9 cups unbleached all-purpose flour

1. Place the grated potato and the 3 cups water in a medium saucepan; bring to a boil over high heat. Reduce the heat, cover, and simmer until the potato pieces are very soft and begin to break apart, 30 to 45 minutes. Remove from the heat.

2. Stir in ¼ cup of the shortening, the sugar, and the salt. Let cool to lukewarm.

3. In a large bowl, sprinkle the yeast over the warm water. When the potato mixture has cooled, add it to the yeast mixture. Add 4 cups of the flour and beat well with a wooden spoon. Gradually add enough of the remaining flour (4 to 5 cups) to make a soft dough. Turn out on a lightly floured surface and knead until smooth and elastic, 5 to 7 minutes.

4. Rinse the bowl with warm water; dry the bowl. Grease the bowl with the remaining 1 teaspoon shortening. Place the ball of dough in the bowl, and turn the dough to grease the top. Cover and let rise until doubled, about 1 hour.

5. Punch down the dough. Divide into 3 parts. Shape each part into a ball and place in well-greased round pans, such as pie tins. Cover and let rise until doubled, about 45 minutes.

6. Meanwhile preheat the oven to 400°F.

7. Sift a light dusting of flour over the risen loaves. Bake in the oven until they are browned on top and sound hollow when tapped on the bottom, 30 to 35 minutes. Cool on wire racks.

Orange–Fennel Rye Bread

Rye doughs benefit from a slow second rising. If the weather is hot and your kitchen is overly warm, place the pans in the refrigerator for the second rising, where the dough will take about 2 hours to rise.

MAKES 2 LOAVES

4 cups bread flour
2 cups medium rye flour
2 teaspoons fennel seeds
2 cups milk, scalded
4 tablespoons (½ stick) unsalted butter, cut into bits
½ cup firmly packed light brown sugar
2 teaspoons salt
¼ cup warm (100° to 105°) water
1 envelope (2¼ teaspoons) active dry yeast (not fast-acting)
1 teaspoon granulated sugar
grated zest of 1 orange
1 tablespoon melted unsalted butter

1. Place both flours and the fennel seeds in a food processor and process to mix the flours and chop the seeds. (Alternately, chop the seeds with a sharp knife and then stir together with the flours.)

2. In a large mixing bowl, stir together the scalded milk, cut-up butter, brown sugar, and salt. Cool to lukewarm.

3. Meanwhile, in a measuring cup, stir together the warm water, yeast, and granulated sugar.

4. When the milk mixture has cooled sufficiently, add the yeast mixture, orange zest, and 4 cups of the flour mixture. Beat well with a

wooden spoon. Gradually add the remaining 2 cups flour to make a soft dough. Toss on a floured surface until no longer sticky. Knead gently until smooth and elastic, 5 to 7 minutes. ·

5. Place the dough in an oiled or greased bowl, turning the dough once to oil the top. Cover with plastic and let rise until doubled, 1 to 1½ hours.

6. Punch down the dough; divide in half. Shape each half into a loaf and place in 2 well-greased 9×5-inch loaf pans. Cover and let rise until doubled, about 1 hour.

7. Meanwhile, preheat the oven to 375°F.

7. Bake the loaves in the oven until they are browned on top and sound hollow when tapped on the bottom, 35 to 40 minutes. Cool on wire racks.

Porch Supper Pan Rolls

This is an easy recipe that makes a nice quantity of rolls in one pan.
MAKES 2 DOZEN

¼ *cup sugar*
¼ *cup solid vegetable shortening*
1 *teaspoon salt*
¾ *cup milk, heated to hot*
¼ *cup warm (100° to 105°) water*
1 *envelope (2¼ teaspoons) active dry yeast (not fast-acting)*
1 *large egg*
3 *to 3½ cups unbleached all-purpose flour*

1. Place the sugar, shortening, and salt in a large mixing bowl. Add the hot milk and stir to dissolve the sugar and the shortening.

2. In a measuring cup, stir together the warm water and yeast. Let the yeast mixture stand while the milk mixture cools.

3. When the milk mixture is lukewarm, stir in the yeast mixture, the egg, and 2 cups of the flour. Beat well with a wooden spoon. Gradually add enough of the remaining 1 to 1½ cups flour to make a soft dough. Turn out on a floured surface and knead until smooth, 3 to 5 minutes.

4. Place the dough in a greased bowl, and turn to coat the top. Cover with plastic wrap and let rise until doubled, about 1 hour.

5. Punch down the dough. Shape into 1½-inch balls (you should have 24) and place in a greased 13×9-inch baking pan (4 across, 6 down). Cover and let rise until almost doubled, about 1 hour.

6. Meanwhile, preheat the oven to 400°F.

7. Bake until the rolls are lightly browned, 20 to 25 minutes. Serve hot.

Old-Fashioned Dinner Rolls

Crescent-shaped rolls have always meant Sunday dinner to me. I make them ahead and freeze them in dozen lots, to take out and use as needed.
MAKES 2 DOZEN

1 cup milk, heated to hot
¼ cup plus 1 teaspoon sugar
4 tablespoons (½ stick) unsalted butter, softened
1¼ teaspoons salt
1 envelope (2¼ teaspoons) active dry yeast (not fast-acting)
¼ cup warm (100° to 105°) water
1 large egg
3½ to 4 cups unbleached all-purpose flour
2 tablespoons melted unsalted butter

1. In a medium mixing bowl, pour the milk over ¼ cup of the sugar, the softened butter, and the salt. Stir to melt the butter. Let cool to warm.

2. Meanwhile, in a small measuring cup, mix the yeast with the warm water and the remaining 1 teaspoon sugar. Let stand until foamy, about 5 minutes.

3. When the milk mixture has cooled to warm, add the yeast mixture, the egg, and 2½ cups of the flour. Beat well with a wooden spoon to form a satiny smooth batter. Add enough of the remaining 1 to 1½ cups flour to make a somewhat sticky dough that leaves the sides of the bowl. Turn out on a lightly floured surface and knead lightly until smooth and elastic, letting the dough pick up only enough flour to prevent sticking.

4. Place the dough in a buttered bowl, and turn once to butter the top. Cover with plastic wrap and let stand until doubled, 1 to 1½ hours.

5. Punch down the dough; divide into 3 parts. Working with 1 part at a time, roll out to a 12-inch circle on a lightly floured surface. Spread with one-third of the melted butter. Cut, as for pie, into 8 equal wedges. Roll each wedge from the wide end to the point and place, point-side down, on a nonstick or greased baking sheet. Curve the ends slightly to form a crescent shape. Cover with plastic wrap and let rise until doubled, about 1 hour.

6. Meanwhile, preheat the oven to 375°F.

7. Bake the rolls in the oven until evenly browned, 12 to 15 minutes. Serve hot.

Pesto-Filled Rolls

Follow the recipe for Old-Fashioned Dinner Rolls. After the first rising and the dividing of the dough, roll each part out to a 12-inch circle, but *do not* spread with melted butter. Instead, drop a small dollop of Pesto (page 139) onto the wide end of each wedge. Roll up and proceed as before.

Pick-Your-Color Corn Bread

You can vary this recipe by using a different color of cornmeal every time you make it.

SERVES 9

1 cup yellow, white, or blue cornmeal, preferably stone-ground
1 cup all-purpose flour
3 tablespoons sugar
1 tablespoon baking powder
½ teaspoon salt
2 large eggs
1 cup milk
3 tablespoons extra-light olive oil

1. Preheat the oven to 425°F. Grease an 8-inch square pan.

2. In a mixing bowl, stir together the cornmeal, flour, sugar, baking powder, and salt. In another bowl, beat the eggs with the milk and oil until smooth. Add the egg mixture to the dry ingredients and stir just until the dry ingredients are moistened; do not overmix.

3. Pour the batter into the prepared pan. Bake until golden brown, 20 to 25 minutes. Serve warm.

Square Soda Biscuits

These old-fashioned biscuits are easy to make. The dough is shaped into a rectangle and the biscuits are cut into squares. No need to worry about what to do with the scraps.

MAKES 1 DOZEN

2 cups all-purpose flour
1 teaspoon baking powder
½ teaspoon baking soda
½ teaspoon salt
½ teaspoon sugar
6 tablespoons (¾ stick) cold unsalted butter, cut into 12 pieces
⅔ cup plus 1 tablespoon buttermilk

1. Preheat the oven to 450°F.

2. In a mixing bowl, whisk together the flour, baking powder, baking soda, salt, and sugar. Cut in the butter with a pastry blender or 2 knives until the mixture resembles coarse cornmeal. Add the buttermilk and stir with a fork just until the dough comes together.

3. Turn out the dough onto a lightly floured surface and toss until no longer sticky. Press into an 8×6-inch rectangle, about ½ inch thick. Cut into a dozen 2-inch squares.

4. Place the squares on an ungreased baking sheet. Bake until golden-brown, 12 to 15 minutes. Serve warm.

Easy Cream Biscuits

The dough for these biscuits is simply stirred with a fork, patted into a rectangle, and cut with a knife. Couldn't be easier.

MAKES 12 BISCUITS

1¾ cups all-purpose flour
1 tablespoon baking powder
½ teaspoon salt
1 cup heavy (whipping) cream

1. Preheat the oven to 450°F.

2. In a mixing bowl, use a fork to stir together the flour, baking powder, and salt. Add the cream and stir with the fork just until the dough comes together. Knead lightly 2 or 3 times in the bowl.

3. Turn out the dough onto a lightly floured surface. Pat into a 6×4½-inch rectangle, about ½ inch thick. Cut into a dozen 1½-inch squares with a knife.

4. Place the squares on an ungreased baking sheet. Bake until lightly browned, 10 to 12 minutes. Serve warm.

Sweet Buttermilk Muffins

At your next family gathering, put these in a bread basket along with the rolls and watch them disappear.

MAKES 18

TOPPING:

1½ tablespoons sugar
¼ teaspoon ground cinnamon

MUFFINS:

8 tablespoons (1 stick) unsalted butter, softened
1 cup sugar
2 large eggs
1 teaspoon pure vanilla extract
2¼ cups all-purpose flour
1 teaspoon baking powder
½ teaspoon baking soda
½ teaspoon salt
½ teaspoon ground cinnamon
¼ teaspoon ground nutmeg
1 cup buttermilk

1. Preheat the oven to 375°F. Line 18 muffin cups with paper liners.

2. Prepare the topping: In a small bowl stir together the 1½ tablespoons sugar and ¼ teaspoon cinnamon. Reserve.

3. Prepare the muffins: In a large mixing bowl, beat the butter until creamy. Add the sugar and beat again. Add the eggs, 1 at a time, beating well after each. Beat in the vanilla.

4. Sift or whisk together the flour, baking powder, baking soda, salt, cinnamon, and nutmeg. Add the dry ingredients to the batter alternately with the buttermilk (3 parts dry, 2 parts buttermilk).

5. Spoon the batter into the paper-lined muffin cups, filling each about two-thirds full. Sprinkle the topping evenly over the tops of the muffins. Bake until lightly browned and a muffin springs back when lightly touched in the center, 18 to 20 minutes.

6. Remove the muffins from the pan as soon as they come from the oven and cool on wire racks. Serve warm or cold.

Desserts

We certainly don't have dessert every day, but when the children come home with their families, we indulge. The grandchildren, of course, expect it. None of the recipes in this chapter are difficult to prepare, but they are part of what keeps my family coming home to share our dinner table.

Deep-Dish Apple Pie with Butterflake Crust is simply spiced to let the flavor of the apples take center stage. The Crustless Peach Pie is a recipe I devised one day when I ran out of time to make a crust for my pie. It was so successful, it has become part of my regular repertoire. Rummy Apple Crisp uses a touch of dark rum to give a little wickedness to an old-fashioned dessert; jarred mincemeat makes an easy stuffing for the Baked Apples with Mincemeat Stuffing; tart rhubarb makes a tasty Rhubarb Dessert Sauce; the square shape of the Rustic Sugar Cookies is easy to accomplish; the Golden and Chocolate Loaf Cakes require no frosting; Serious Brownies are sinfully chocolate; and Hot Fudge Ice Cream Puffs are a pure delight.

Deep-Dish Apple Pie with Butterflake Crust

Tart apples have a wonderful flavor of their own. The spices used here enhance rather than cover up that virtue. Make the easy food processor dough for the crust first to allow time for chilling while you prepare the apples.

SERVES 8

BUTTERFLAKE CRUST:

1½ cups all-purpose flour
¼ teaspoon salt
1 teaspoon granulated sugar
8 tablespoons (1 stick) cold unsalted butter, cut into 8 pieces
1 large egg yolk, cold
1 teaspoon fresh lemon juice
about 2 tablespoons cold water

FILLING:

8 cups peeled, cored, and sliced tart cooking apples (about 4
   pounds)
2 tablespoons fresh lemon juice
¾ cup granulated sugar
¾ cup firmly packed light brown sugar
3 tablespoons cornstarch
1 teaspoon ground cinnamon
¼ teaspoon ground nutmeg
2 tablespoons unsalted butter, slivered

1. Prepare the crust: Place the flour, salt, and sugar in a food processor fitted with the metal blade. Pulse to mix. Scatter the butter in a circle on top of the flour mixture. Pulse on and off until the butter is reduced to flakes.

2. In a measuring cup, beat the egg yolk, lemon juice, and cold water with a fork. Pour in a circle over the butter-flour mixture. Pulse just long enough to mix and begin to bring the dough together. Add additional water, 1 teaspoon at a time, if the mixture appears dry and crumbly. Do not expect the dough to form a ball.

3. Turn out the dough onto a large piece of waxed paper and pat into a disk about 6 inches in diameter. Wrap the dough in the waxed paper and refrigerate for at least 20 minutes before rolling out.

4. Meanwhile, preheat the oven to 425°F.

5. Roll out the crust: Tear off two 12-inch squares of waxed paper. Place the dough on one piece of paper and cover with the other.

Press gently on the top piece of paper. Roll out from the center to the outside edges to make a circle one-inch larger than the diameter of the dish it will cover (the dough should be about ¼ inch thick).

6. Prepare the filling: Butter a 2½- to 3-quart shallow casserole or deep pie dish. Put the prepared apples into a large bowl. Sprinkle with the lemon juice and toss to coat. In another bowl, stir together the white and brown sugars, the cornstarch, cinnamon, and nutmeg. Sprinkle the sugar mixture over the apples and toss to coat. Transfer the apples to the buttered dish. Dot the top of the apples with the slivered butter. Cover with the rolled-out crust. Cut several vents for steam. Crimp the edges of the crust, but do not seal it to the edge of the dish.

7. Bake until the filling is bubbling and the top is well-browned, 45 to 50 minutes.

Serving suggestion: Serve warm or cold, spooned into bowls and topped with vanilla ice cream.

Crustless Peach Pie

If you don't mind doing without a crust, you'll love this peach dessert.
SERVES 6

5 cups peeled, sliced peaches
½ cup granulated sugar
⅓ cup plus 2 tablespoons all-purpose flour
½ teaspoon ground cinnamon
1 teaspoon fresh lemon juice
½ cup firmly packed light brown sugar
3 tablespoons unsalted butter

1. Preheat the oven to 375°F.

2. In a mixing bowl, toss the peaches with the sugar, 2 tablespoons of the flour, and the cinnamon. Place in an 8-inch square glass baking dish; sprinkle the lemon juice over the peaches.

3. In a bowl, stir together the brown sugar and the remaining ⅓ cup flour. Cut in the butter to make crumbs. Sprinkle the crumbs over the peaches.

4. Bake until the filling is bubbling and the topping is lightly browned, about 35 minutes.

Serving suggestion: Spoon into bowls and top with cream or ice cream.

Rummy Apple Crisp

When we vacation in Michigan, we sometimes find wild apple trees in the woods which we harvest to make this crisp. I'm convinced they were planted by Johnny Appleseed.

SERVES 6

6 cups peeled, thinly sliced tart apples
2 tablespoons dark rum
½ cup all-purpose flour
¼ cup granulated sugar
¼ cup firmly packed light brown sugar
⅛ teaspoon salt
½ teaspoon ground cinnamon
⅛ teaspoon ground nutmeg
4 tablespoons (½ stick) unsalted butter

1. Preheat the oven to 375°F.

2. Butter an 8-inch square baking pan. Fill the pan with the sliced apples; sprinkle with the rum.

3. In a medium bowl, stir together the flour, white and brown sugars, the salt, cinnamon, and nutmeg. Cut in the butter to make crumbs. Sprinkle the crumb mixture over the apples.

4. Bake until lightly browned and bubbly, about 30 minutes.

Serving suggestion: Serve warm or cold, topped with vanilla ice cream.

Baked Apples with Mincemeat Stuffing

Raisins with cinnamon-sugar need not be the only choice for stuffing a baked apple. Mincemeat, laced with cognac, has more adventuresome appeal. Use already prepared mincemeat, packed in a jar, for ease of preparation.

SERVES 4

1 cup prepared mincemeat
2 tablespoons cognac or brandy
4 large Red Rome apples
¼ cup apple juice
2 tablespoons unsalted butter, slivered

1. Preheat the oven to 375°F. Butter an 8-inch square pan or glass baking dish.

2. In a bowl, stir together the mincemeat and cognac.

3. Core the apples, starting at the stem end and stopping just short of the base. Pare away a ½-inch strip of peel around the stem end. Stuff the apples with the mincemeat mixture.

4. Place the apples in the buttered dish. Mix any remaining stuffing with the apple juice; pour the juice mixture around the apples. Dot the tops of the apples and the sauce with the slivered butter.

5. Bake until the apples feel soft when pierced with a fork, 40 to 45 minutes.

Serving suggestion: Place an apple in each serving dish. Spoon the sauce around the apples. Pass a pitcher of milk or cream.

Rhubarb Dessert Sauce

We pull the first stalks from our rhubarb patch during the latter part of April, and consider the tart sauce they make to be nature's spring tonic.

MAKES 3 CUPS, SERVES 4 TO 6

1 cup sugar
¼ teaspoon ground ginger
4 cups thinly sliced rhubarb
¼ cup cool water

1. *To cook on stovetop:* In a nonreactive medium saucepan, stir together the sugar and ginger. Add the rhubarb, and stir in the water. Bring to a simmer over medium heat. Cook, stirring often, until the rhubarb is soft, about 2 minutes. *To cook in a microwave oven:* Stir together the sugar and ginger in a microwave-safe dish. Add the rhubarb and water. Cover and cook on high for 2 minutes. Stir. Cook for 1 minute longer; stir. Continue to cook, stirring at 1-minute intervals, until the rhubarb is tender.

2. Let the sauce cool to room temperature. Cover and refrigerate for up to 1 week.

Serving suggestion: Spoon this sauce over ice cream or unfrosted cake or use as an accompaniment to the Rustic Sugar Cookies.

Rustic Sugar Cookies

These are easy to mix and bake. Simply roll out and cut into squares, leaving no scraps to mess with. The baked cookies are charmingly rustic.

MAKES 3 DOZEN

1 cup sugar, plus more for sprinkling on the cookies
½ cup white vegetable shortening
1 large egg
1 tablespoon pure vanilla extract
2 tablespoons milk
2 cups all-purpose flour
¼ teaspoon salt
1 teaspoon baking powder

1. In a large mixing bowl, gradually add the sugar to the shortening, beating until light and fluffy. Add the egg and beat again. Stir in the vanilla and the milk. Stir together the flour, salt, and baking powder; stir into the dough. Cover and chill the dough until firm, about 1 hour.

2. Preheat the oven to 375°F. Use ungreased baking sheets.

3. Divide the dough into 3 pieces. One at a time, roll out the dough on a lightly floured surface into a 12×9-inch rectangle. Cut into a dozen 3-inch squares. Transfer to the baking sheets, leaving 1 inch between them. (It doesn't matter if the edges of the cookies are uneven.) Sprinkle a light, even coating of sugar on the tops of the cookies.

4. Bake until browned on the edges with a few lightly browned patches on top, about 8 minutes. Transfer to wire racks to cool. Roll out, cut, and bake the remaining cookies.

5. If they don't get eaten right away, store any remaining cookies airtight.

Golden Loaf Cake

Loaf cakes are easy because they require no frosting. Slices spread with softened butter make great cake sandwiches for picnics.

SERVES 8 TO 12

8 tablespoons (1 stick) unsalted butter, softened
1 cup sugar
2 large eggs
1 teaspoon pure vanilla extract
1½ cups all-purpose flour
2 teaspoons baking powder
¼ teaspoon salt
¼ teaspoon ground nutmeg
½ cup milk

1. Preheat the oven to 350°F. Grease and flour a 9×5-inch loaf pan.

2. Beat the butter until smooth. Gradually add the sugar, beating until light and fluffy. Add the eggs, 1 at a time, beating well after each. Stir in the vanilla. Sift or whisk together the flour, baking powder, salt, and nutmeg. Add the flour mixture alternately with the milk, beating well after each addition (3 parts flour mixture, 2 parts milk). Pour the batter into the prepared pan.

3. Bake until a wooden toothpick inserted in the center comes out clean, 45 to 50 minutes.

4. Cool in the pan for 5 minutes. Turn out on a wire rack to cool completely.

Chocolate Loaf Cake

We like to use slices of this cake as a foundation for building ice cream sundaes.

SERVES 8 TO 12

8 tablespoons (1 stick) unsalted butter, softened
½ cup granulated sugar
½ cup firmly packed light brown sugar
2 large eggs
½ teaspoon pure vanilla extract
1¾ cups all-purpose flour
½ cup unsweetened cocoa powder
1 teaspoon baking powder
½ teaspoon baking soda
½ teaspoon salt
½ teaspoon ground cinnamon
1 cup buttermilk

1. Preheat the oven to 350°F. Grease and flour a 9×5-inch loaf pan.

2. In a large mixing bowl, beat the butter until smooth. Add the granulated sugar and beat again; add the brown sugar and beat again. Add the eggs, 1 at a time, beating well after each. Beat in the vanilla. Sift or whisk together the flour, cocoa, baking powder, baking soda, salt, and cinnamon. Add the dry ingredients to the batter alternately with the buttermilk, mixing well after each addition (3 parts dry ingredients, 2 parts buttermilk).

3. Scrape the batter into the prepared pan. Bake until a wooden toothpick inserted in the center comes out clean, 50 to 60 minutes.

4. Cool in the pan for 5 minutes. Turn out on a wire rack to cool completely.

Serving suggestion: Top slices of cake with scoops of vanilla ice cream, pour hot fudge sauce over both cake and cream. Sprinkle your favorite nuts on top.

Serious Brownies

These have enough chocolate to please even me. You can snack on them at any time of day, but I save mine for after supper, when I top them with a scoop of vanilla ice cream.

MAKES 2 DOZEN

6 squares (1 ounce each) unsweetened chocolate, chopped
12 tablespoons (1½ sticks) unsalted butter, cut up
2 cups granulated sugar
3 large eggs
¼ teaspoon salt
2 teaspoons pure vanilla extract
1 cup all-purpose flour
1 cup chopped pecans

FROSTING:
1½ cups confectioners' sugar
¼ cup unsweetened cocoa powder
pinch of salt
3 tablespoons unsalted butter, softened
½ teaspoon pure vanilla extract
2 to 3 tablespoons hot coffee or milk

1. Preheat the oven to 350°F. Grease a 13×9-inch baking pan.

2. In a microwave-safe mixing bowl, combine the chocolate and butter. Microwave on HIGH until melted and smooth when stirred, 1½ to 2 minutes.

3. Add the sugar and beat until well blended. Add the eggs, 1 at a time, beating well after each. Stir in the salt and vanilla. Stir in the flour just until mixed. Fold in the pecans. Spread the batter evenly in the prepared pan.

4. Bake in the oven until the brownies just begin to pull away from the edges of the pan, 22 to 25 minutes. Place on a rack to cool while preparing the frosting.

5. Prepare the frosting: In a small mixing bowl, stir together the powdered sugar, cocoa powder, and salt. (If there are lumps in the sugar or cocoa, you may want to stir the mixture through a sieve.) Add the butter, vanilla, and 2 tablespoons of the liquid; stir to mix. Add additional liquid if needed to make the mixture spreadable. Spread the frosting on the warm brownies. Wait until the brownies are completely cooled before cutting into squares.

Simple Vanilla Ice Cream

This easy ice cream is made from sweetened cream and vanilla extract with no additives to detract from the flavor. You can substitute light cream or half-and-half for up to 2 cups of the cream called for to produce an ice cream with less butterfat. You could also use all light cream, but the results are more like an ice milk than a frozen cream.

MAKES ABOUT 1½ QUARTS

4 cups heavy (whipping) cream
1 cup sugar
1 tablespoon pure vanilla extract

1. In a mixing bowl, gently stir together the cream and sugar until the sugar dissolves. Stir in the vanilla.

2. Process in an ice cream freezer according to the manufacturer's instructions.

Wooden Spoon Kitchen Wisdom:
About Freezing Ice Cream

Mixtures containing a high butterfat cream should be well chilled before loading into an ice cream churn. A warm mixture requires too much churning action before freezing takes place, producing an undesirable buttery texture in the finished ice cream.

Hot Fudge Ice Cream Puffs

Cream puff batter is easy to make and the puffs, combined with ice cream and hot fudge, make a very special dessert.

SERVES 6

PUFFS:

½ *cup water*
4 *tablespoons (½ stick) unsalted butter*
pinch of salt
½ *cup all-purpose flour*
2 *large eggs*

HOT FUDGE SAUCE:

¼ *cup milk*
2 *tablespoons unsalted butter*
dash of salt
1 *cup (6 ounces) semisweet chocolate morsels*

1 *pint vanilla ice cream*
confectioners' sugar, for dusting the puffs

1. Preheat the oven to 350°F. Line a baking sheet with parchment paper. (If you don't have parchment paper, lightly grease the sheet.)

2. Prepare the puffs: In a small saucepan, heat the water, butter, and salt over high heat until the butter melts and the water boils. Reduce the heat to medium, and add the flour all at once. Stirring constantly, cook until the mixture forms a ball that leaves the sides of the pan, about 1 minute. Remove the pan from the heat and let cool for 5 minutes.

3. Add the eggs, 1 at a time, beating well with a wooden spoon after each addition until the mixture is smooth.

4. Drop the batter, making 6 round globs, onto the parchment paper, spacing them 3 inches apart. Bake until golden-brown, 30 to 35 minutes. Cool on a wire rack.

5. Meanwhile, prepare the hot fudge: In a small saucepan over medium heat, combine the milk, butter, and salt, stirring until the butter melts. Reduce the heat to low, add the chocolate, and cook, stirring constantly, until the mixture is smooth. Remove from the heat and keep warm.

Serving suggestion: Slice the tops from the puffs and remove any soft dough from inside. Fill the puffs with scoops of the vanilla ice cream. Replace the tops. Spoon the hot fudge over the top. Lightly dust powdered sugar over all.

Brown Sugar Bread Pudding with Apricot Sauce

You can use either white or light wheat bread in this old-fashioned bread pudding. The flavor is wonderful.

SERVES 6

BREAD PUDDING:

*4 to 5 slices soft bread, crusts removed and cubed (you should
have 4 cups bread cubes)*
2½ cups milk
½ cup golden raisins
2 tablespoons unsalted butter
3 large eggs
¼ cup granulated sugar
¼ cup firmly packed light brown sugar
¼ teaspoon salt
¼ teaspoon ground nutmeg
2 teaspoons pure vanilla extract

APRICOT SAUCE:

¾ cup apricot preserves
1 tablespoon fresh lemon juice
1 tablespoon unsalted butter

1. Preheat the oven to 350°F.

2. Prepare the pudding: Place the bread cubes in a heavy 2-quart casserole dish. In a medium saucepan over medium heat, combine the milk, raisins, and butter. Cook, stirring now and then, until the milk is hot and the butter melts. Remove from the heat.

3. In a mixing bowl, beat the eggs until smooth. Add the white and brown sugars, the salt, and nutmeg and beat again until smooth. Add about ½ cup of the hot milk mixture to the egg mixture and stir until mixed. Gradually stir in the remaining milk mixture. Stir in the vanilla. Pour the combined mixture over the bread cubes. Stir well to disperse the raisins and to ensure that all bread cubes are moistened.

4. Bake in the oven until a table knife inserted halfway between the center and the edge of the custard comes out clean, about 40 minutes. Remove from the oven to cool slightly while preparing the sauce.

5. Combine the preserves, lemon juice, and butter in a nonreactive small saucepan. Stir over medium heat until the mixture is warm and the butter melts.

Serving suggestion: Spoon the warm bread pudding into serving dishes. Spoon the apricot sauce over the top of the pudding. Serve any extra sauce in a sauceboat at the table.

Cup Custard

This old-fashioned custard is wonderful.
SERVES 4

2 cups light cream or half-and-half
⅓ cup sugar
⅛ teaspoon salt
2 large eggs
1 large egg yolk
1½ teaspoons pure vanilla extract

freshly grated nutmeg
boiling water

1. Preheat the oven to 350°F. Place 4 ramekins in a shallow baking pan.

2. Heat the cream until hot but not boiling. Remove from the heat. Add the sugar and salt and stir to dissolve.

3. In a small mixing bowl, whisk the eggs and egg yolk until smooth. Add the hot cream mixture, about 2 tablespoons at a time, stirring gently but well with each addition. (The slow incorporation of the hot cream prevents the eggs from curdling; the gentle stirring prevents a froth from forming on top of the custard.) Stir in the vanilla. Divide the custard among the ramekins. Sprinkle the nutmeg over the tops.

4. Place the baking pan on the oven rack. Pour boiling water into the pan to reach 1 inch up the sides of the ramekins. Bake until a knife inserted in the center of the custard comes out clean, about 30 minutes. Best served slightly warm, but leftovers should be refrigerated and served cold.

Soft White Chocolate Pudding

Soft pudding was one of the "get-well" foods my mother used to make for me when I was sick. I liked it so well that I sometimes feigned illness in an effort to trick her into making it. Think what I would have done if she had thought to put white chocolate in hers.

SERVES 4

>2 *cups milk*
>4 *ounces white chocolate, such as Ghiradelli's, chopped or*
>   *broken into small pieces*
>3 *large eggs*
>⅓ *cup sugar*
>⅛ *teaspoon salt*
>1 *teaspoon pure vanilla extract*

1. In a small saucepan, over medium-high heat, heat the milk until hot. Reduce the heat to low, stir in the white chocolate and heat, stirring constantly, until it melts, 5 to 7 minutes. Remove from the heat.

2. In a nonreactive large saucepan, combine the eggs, sugar, and salt; beat until smooth. Pour about 2 tablespoons of the hot milk mixture into the egg mixture and stir until well combined. Continue in this fashion until all is incorporated.

3. Place the pan over medium heat and cook, stirring constantly, until the mixture thickens enough to coat a metal spoon, about 10 minutes. Do not allow to boil. If it threatens to do so, reduce the heat. Remove from the heat when thickened.

4. Stir in the vanilla. Let the custard cool to lukewarm; stir occasionally to release steam. Pour into serving dishes and refrigerate until chilled.

Selected Bibliography

When I am interviewed, the questioner invariably decides that I am self-taught. I find that term misleading. Building on the foundation laid in my mother's kitchen, I continue to learn by listening to good cooks discuss their successes and failures and by studying the writings of others. I list here my most valued resources, with the recommendation that you include them on your cookbook shelf:

Child, Julia. *The Way to Cook.* New York: Alfred A. Knopf, 1989.

Cunningham, Marion. *The Fannie Farmer Cookbook.* Twelfth edition. New York: Alfred A. Knopf, 1979.

Larousse Gastronomique. London: The Hamlyn Publishing Group Limited, 1988.

McGee, Harold. *On Food and Cooking.* New York: Charles Scribner's Sons, 1984.

Rombauer, Irma S., and Marion Rombauer Becker. *Joy of Cooking.* Indianapolis: Bobbs-Merrill Company, 1975.

Willan, Anne. *La Varenne Pratique.* New York: Crown Publishers, 1989.

Worth, Helen. *Cooking Without Recipes.* New York: Harper & Row, 1965.

Index